THE INDEPENDENT NEUROPSYCHOLOGICAL EVALUATION

OXFORD WORKSHOP SERIES

AMERICAN ACADEMY OF CLINICAL NEUROPSYCHOLOGY

Series Editors

Volumes in the Series

Ethical Decision Making in Clinical Neuropsychology
Shane S. Bush

Mild Traumatic Brain Injury and Postconcussion Syndrome
Michael A. McCrea

Understanding Somatization in the Practice of Clinical Neuropsychology
Greg J. Lamberty

Board Certification in Clinical Neuropsychology
Kira E. Armstrong, Dean W. Beebe, Robin C. Hilsabeck, Michael W. Kirkwood

Adult Learning Disabilities and ADHD
Robert L. Mapou

Neuropsychology of Epilepsy and Eplilepsy Surgery
Gregory P. Lee

The Business of Neuropsychology
Mark T. Barisa

Mild Cognitive Impairment and Dementia
Glenn E. Smith and Mark W. Bondi

Intellectual Disability: Civil and Criminal Forensic Issues
Michael Chafetz

Executive Functioning: A Comprehensive Guide for Clinical Practice
Yana Suchy

The Independent Neuropsychological Evaluation
Howard J. Oakes, David W. Lovejoy, and Shane S. Bush

AACN
American Academy of
Clinical Neuropsychology

THE INDEPENDENT NEUROPSYCHOLOGICAL EVALUATION

Howard J. Oakes, PsyD
David W. Lovejoy, PsyD
Shane S. Bush, PhD

OXFORD WORKSHOP SERIES

OXFORD
UNIVERSITY PRESS

OXFORD
UNIVERSITY PRESS

Oxford University Press is a department of the University of Oxford. It furthers the University's objective of excellence in research, scholarship, and education by publishing worldwide. Oxford is a registered trade mark of Oxford University Press in the UK and certain other countries.

Published in the United States of America by Oxford University Press
198 Madison Avenue, New York, NY 10016, United States of America.

Library of Congress Cataloging-in-Publication Data
Names: Oakes, Howard J., author. | Lovejoy, David W., author. |
Bush, Shane S., 1965– author. | American Academy of Clinical Neuropsychology.
Title: The independent neuropsychological evaluation / Howard J. Oakes,
David W. Lovejoy, Shane S. Bush.
Description: New York, NY : Oxford University Press, 2017. |
Series: Oxford workshop series | Includes bibliographical references and index.
Identifiers: LCCN 2016048987 (print) | LCCN 2016049935 (ebook) |
ISBN 9780199828326 (pbk. : alk. paper) | ISBN 9780190682040 (UPDF) |
ISBN 9780190682057 (EPUB)
Subjects: | MESH: Neuropsychology—organization & administration |
Neuropsychological Tests
Classification: LCC RC386.6.N48 (print) | LCC RC386.6.N48 (ebook) | NLM WL
103.5 | DDC 616.8/0475—dc23
LC record available at https://lccn.loc.gov/2016048987

H. J. O.: To Claudia and Jim. Thank you for your support.

D. W. L.: To Isabel and Jack, for all you mean to me.

S. S. B.: To Dana, Sarah, and Megan, who inspire me in all that I do.

Contents

Preface

The competent practice of clinical neuropsychology requires an ongoing process of education, training, and consultation. For many practitioners, evolving clinical practice involves an increasing variety of referral sources, patient populations, and referral questions. The exponential growth of neuropsychological services in the medico-legal and disability arenas over the past several decades has created more exposure to practice issues in these arenas for neuropsychologists.

Although the subject matter covered in this book has relevance to neuropsychological independent medical evaluations (IMEs) conducted in the context of civil litigation, workers' compensation, fitness for duty, and state or federally sponsored disability programs, this book emphasizes IMEs conducted for private disability insurance companies. In writing this book, we draw upon decades of combined experience conducting and reviewing IMEs for many of the country's largest private disability insurers.

It is in this context that we hope to provide insights into the basic framework for conducting IMEs. We believe that the information contained in this book will have relevance for the novice IME provider, as well as providers who have greater levels of experience and expertise in this area. The information covered throughout this text should also have cross-disciplinary relevance for IME providers in related fields such as neurology and psychiatry who may struggle with some of the same disability-related issues and questions during IMEs.

It is our goal that this text will provide clarity regarding some of the complex issues associated with disability-related assessments by explaining the language and context of "disability," relevant ethical and professional considerations, and business aspects of IMEs, as well as particular neuropsychological-related issues. It is our hope that providers of IMEs (as well as those who contribute information via other avenues for consideration in the adjudication of disability claims) will share a common understanding that results in a professional product that is useful, reliable, and valid for this purpose.

We are deeply indebted to the American Academy of Clinical Neuropsychology (AACN) and the Oxford Workshop Series team, particularly Joan Bossert and Lynnee Argabright, for their patience and belief that this topic was worthy of inclusion in such a series of wonderful and important works that have preceded ours. Although we have benefited from our experiences within the clinical world, the forensic arena, and the disability industry, it is important for us to be clear that the observations, views, and opinions that are offered in this text are our own and do not reflect policy, procedures, or practices associated with any academic institution, clinical facility, or disability carrier. We remain committed to the value of independent neuropsychological evaluations that are indeed independent, professionally sound, ethically administered, comprehensive in their scope, and useful in terms of their opinions.

THE INDEPENDENT NEUROPSYCHOLOGICAL EVALUATION

1

Introduction

There are clear indications that rates of disability claims have been increasing over the past several decades. A 20-year-old person is estimated to have a 30% chance of becoming disabled over the course of his or her work life (US Social Security Administration, 2003). Estimates have also indicated that approximately 12.6% of Americans in 2013 were identified as having a disability. This equates to approximately 39 million non-institutionalized individuals currently in the United States (Erickson, Lee, & von Schrader, 2015). The etiologic underpinnings of this phenomenon are thought to be multifactorial and include socioeconomic variables such as aging, national employment rates, family support, and changing legislative and definitional criteria. The latest economic crisis has added another facet to this already complicated picture, with the ranks of those receiving Social Security Disability benefits increasing by an additional 2 million individuals from 2006 to 2014 (US Social Security Administration, 2015).

From a behavioral health perspective, recent concerns about increasing rates of disability have been particularly salient. A study conducted by the World Health Organization, World Bank, and Harvard University reported that there has been a long-standing tendency to underestimate the burden caused by mental illness in relation to both health and productivity (Murray & Lopez, 1996). The study found that mental illness accounts for over 15% of the burden of disease (both direct and indirect costs) in established market communities such as the United States. Placing this statistic in perspective, it represents a greater disease burden than combining all forms of cancer. Moreover, the study reported that depression is expected to become the leading cause of global disability by the year 2020. Insurance industry statistics related to behavioral health disability claims within the United States have also indicated that there has been a significant increase in such claims. Hurrell and Murphy (1996) observed that claims associated with mental stress composed the fastest-growing segment of work-related illness. Statistics from California further reveal that claims related to work stress increased 700% from 1979 to 1988 (California Workers' Compensation Institute, 1990). Warren (2005) also reported a greater than 300% increase in overall behavioral health claims in the prior decade. More recent research suggests some leveling off of the growth of the percentage of mental health–related claims in private disability (Council for Disability Awareness, 2014). Further, the medical and scientific communities have experienced significant expansion related to research and clinical understanding associated with behavioral health conditions. This proliferation has been broadly evident through emphases on the "Decade of the Brain," followed by the more recent "Decade of Behavior," the human genome project, and the proliferation of functional neuroimaging techniques (e.g., SPECT, PET, and fMRI) in understanding how behavioral health conditions are manifested and most optimally treated.

Despite growing insights in relation to the identification, diagnosis, and treatment of these conditions, the current corpus of research lacks appropriate depth to help in further elucidating direct relationships between clinical impairment and occupational disability for any particular behavioral health or physical condition. For instance, research has found that, at any particular time, roughly 45% of actively employed individuals suffer from conditions potentially severe enough to warrant the filing of a work-related disability claim (Biddle, Roberts, Rosenman, & Welch, 1998). Disability statistics indicate that the majority of the individuals who are actively suffering from physical or emotional discomfort adapt and persevere in their jobs and their lives, without making a claim of disability (Biddle et al., 1998). Findings such as these underscore an important multifactorial question within the field of disability that empirical research has not yet been able to clarify: that is, how do clinical, personality, social, financial, legal, and political variables combine in a comprehensive fashion for any one person to create a disability? At a basic level, statistics such as these also emphasize the inappropriateness of conceptual models that assume a direct or linear relationship between the simple presence of a symptom or disorder and the downstream experience of work-related impairment and/or disability.

The sociological, psychological, and medical literatures are replete with studies that identify a myriad of predictor variables associated with the risk and potential maintenance of work-related impairment and/or disability. Demographic factors, psychosocial factors, economic factors, contractual and/or entitlement definitions, personality factors, job satisfaction, and symptom presentation have all been identified as possible contributors to complaints of persistent impairment and/or disability (Franche, Frank, & Krause, 2005). Unfortunately, the specific roles, relative contributions, and interactions among these variables, in the development and long-term maintenance of work-related impairments and/or disability, remain poorly understood. Emerging from this body of literature, however, is a clear understanding that a focus on both external and intra-individual variables will likely offer the most complete picture of who may be most vulnerable to developing a disability. Additionally, available explanatory models have not yet proved efficacious in the development and initiation of protocols and methods for early identification, intervention, and treatment for those at risk for persistent disability-related difficulties. As a result, the growing costs to compensation systems (public and private), legal systems, health care, work sites (especially in relation to lost productivity), and society as a whole continue to increase.

Claims for disability benefits related to behavioral health conditions may be viewed as particularly challenging for those attempting to adjudicate such claims (Piechowski, 2015; Waldron, 2003). In addition to the difficulties associated with understanding how multiple factors interact to predict a general picture of disability, authors (Hadjistavropoulos & Bieling, 2001; Piechowski, 2006) have noted that the subjective nature of behavioral health complaints also contributes to the overall challenge in evaluating such claims. Indeed, there remains no litmus test or lab assay to determine the existence or nonexistence of a behavioral health condition. There are also no clear empirically based guidelines or models for reliably establishing the degree of occupational impairment associated with behavioral health conditions based on diagnosis alone.

The definitional concept of "disability" differs across settings. For instance, the definition used to determine disability may differ across private and public entities. Moreover, it is possible for both entities to offer multiple contracts, each with a different definition of "disability." As disability typically represents a contractual or legal concept, the presence of "disability" is not established by a behavioral health specialist (nor should it be). Instead, the behavioral health specialist serves as a source of information for those seeking to determine "disability." As such, behavioral health specialists providing input to the disability determination process are well advised to be familiar with the context in which this occurs.

Understanding the Context

The availability of insurance to guard against loss of income from sickness or injury dates back to the mid-nineteenth century, when injury insurance was added to the price of railway tickets in England (Cox, 1949). This idea quickly spread to the United States and has evolved over the past century with the introduction of both private and government-sponsored products. At the current time, there are three primary sources of disability-related insurance for working Americans: Social Security Disability Insurance (SSDI), Workers' Compensation, and private disability plans. Another major source of disability-related benefits is the Veterans Administration (VA), which provides benefits to approximately 4 million veterans for service-related injuries and illness (US Department of Veterans Affairs, 2011). In light of its unique context and disability determination process, the VA system it is not discussed in detail in this text. However, much of the information in subsequent chapters will likely be of relevance to those who provide evaluations and opinions within the context of VA-related disability determination. Also, while not the focus of this text, issues particular to SSDI as well as Workers' Compensation are discussed in the following.

US Social Security Administration

The Social Security Act of 1935 established both the Supplemental Security Income and Social Security Disability Income (SSDI) programs. The former is a need-based program based on income rather than on disability status (though it may also be available to those who are disabled). The intent of SSDI is to provide cash assistance to those who suffer severe injuries or illness that render them permanently and completely disabled. Eligibility is based on having made contributions to the Social Security trust fund through earnings over multiple years.

Unlike private disability or workers' compensation insurance, there is not variation from state to state with respect to the definition of disability. For SSDI, the definition of disability is an "inability to engage in any substantial gainful activity by reason of any medically determinable physical or mental impairment which can be expected to result in death or which has lasted or can be expected to last for a continuous period of not less than 12 months" (42 USC §423(d) (1) (A)) (US Government Publishing Office, 2006).

SSDI is administered at the state level through various Disability Determination Services agencies. The evaluation of disability follows a stepwise progression of first establishing diagnosis and then determining the resulting functional impairment for this condition or combined conditions. As noted earlier, the number of individuals with ongoing SSDI claims has climbed significantly over the past decade; currently the two largest impairment categories for SSDI are "mental disorders" and musculoskeletal disorders.

Workers' Compensation

In the industrial revolution of the nineteenth century, workplace injuries were common and frequently resulted in employees who were no longer able to work and who had no resources to care for themselves. Workers' compensation laws were instituted that set liability for workplace injuries on the employer, while at the same time reducing access for employees to other legal remedies to be compensated for their injuries. The critical test factor was the relationship of any injury to the performance of one's work duties. As such, causation remains a critical factor in the determination of benefits. Workers' compensation plans are regulated at the state level but may be administered by private or quasi-private agencies, depending on the state. The exception is for federal employees who are covered by the Federal Employee's Compensation Act, which is administered under the Department of Labor.

Private Disability Insurance

Private disability insurance is a thriving market, with products offered as an employee benefit or to individuals seeking independently to protect their livelihood in case of accident or illness. Individual disability insurance can be offered through plans available to specific professional groups or organizations, or to individuals who may or may not be covered through other plans. Employer-provided plans may differ significantly from plans offered to individuals by the type of coverage provided, the underwriting process, benefits and time frame of benefits provided, as well as the types of regulations (at either the state or federal level) that guide the administration of these plans. The following is a discussion of some of these differences.

Underwriting

Private insurers seek to manage their risk through a variety of means. One significant tool is understanding and accounting for the rates of injury and illness within groups for whom coverage is offered. In employer-provided plans, insurers seek to manage risk by having a diverse pool of insureds, as well as understanding the potential risk that may be present within a specific employee group. For example, employers with a large pool of employees who have heavy physical demands may be at greater risk for orthopedic-related claims and permanent disability arising from these conditions. Premiums are then adjusted to account for this risk.

For individual insurance, insurers are duly concerned about individual risk factors for suffering a later disabling condition. As such, the need to evaluate a particular individual's risk factors, including both personal health history and current occupation, are needed in order to appreciate the risk that may be present. Unlike group-offered plans in which any single individual's health history has little impact on the overall risk profile of a pool of employees, those offering individual insurance seek medical information at the time of application to determine risk at an individual level. Depending on the risk present, policy language may be adjusted to either exclude from coverage preexisting conditions or to limit benefit periods for certain conditions, or the pricing of the policy may be adjusted in an effort to account for increased risk.

Benefits

In group-sponsored plans, benefits are most often defined by a percentage of pre-disability income. Benefits may also be reduced (through policy language) based on the duration of a disabling condition, and/or the definition of what constitutes a disabling condition may change over the course of a claim. For example, many group plans provide coverage for one's occupation for two years but then base coverage on one's ability to perform any occupation for which the individual has the education, experience, and training to perform after that time.

For individual plans, the amount of coverage is selected by the policyholder but is constrained by their previous income history. Increasing coverage corresponds with increasing premiums. Many of these policies allow for selecting increased coverage as income grows throughout one's professional life.

Policy Language

While regulated at state and federal levels, there is a wide range of policies in both the individual and group markets, both across and within various insurers. Further, specific policy language is an evolving process within insurers who seek to manage their risk based on previous experience by adapting language in newer policies. For example, many older policies delineated between "organic" versus "non-organic" causes of disability in defining benefits. At the time this language was being employed, this was considered an adequate way to convey medically versus psychiatrically based causes of impairment. Over time, the inherent limitations of this language to effectively differentiate between psychiatric- and non-psychiatric-based claims (which do carry different types of morbidity) became evident, and policy language evolved (over a series of iterations). It is now more common to seek delineation between conditions included in the *Diagnostic and Statistical Manual of Mental Disorders* (DSM) (in its current form, currently the fifth edition; American Psychiatric Association, 2013) versus those not included in the DSM (often with some specific exceptions noted).

It is of the utmost importance for the independent medical evaluation (IME) provider to be aware that an evaluation of a claimant falls squarely in the context of the specific language of the specific policy that is in force at the time of the evaluation. It is also of importance to be aware that the role of the IME provider is not to determine disability, but rather to provide a work product that facilitates the application of the policy language to the condition and potential impairments present. As such, the following provides some exemplars of terms often included in a disability policy.

Elimination Period

This refers to the time period that an individual must be out of work before becoming eligible for benefits. For group policies, this time period may be as short as a week. For individual policies, it is more common to have a 90-day elimination period. The length of the elimination period has a significant influence on the pricing of a policy, with greater cost for shorter periods. Clearly the longer the elimination period, the less likely an individual is to suffer from a continuous period of impairment, and significantly fewer diseases or conditions are likely to cause functional impairment at 90 days versus at 7 days.

Occupation

As many policies offer coverage in specific relation to one's occupation, policy language defines what is meant by "occupation." For private disability, this generally reflects the specific duties being performed at the time an individual became "disabled," though for some policies it may reflect a general occupational class. As an example, the occupation class of "psychologist" would cover a wide range of potential work-related duties, whereas an individual within that class may be performing a very limited range of actual duties (i.e., providing only therapy, doing only testing). The following are some exemplars of definitions of occupation:

Own occupation: Total disability is an inability to perform the primary duties of one's occupation because of an injury or sickness.

Any occupation: Total disability is the inability to perform the primary duties associated with any occupation for which the individual is qualified by education, training, and/or experience.

Catastrophic disability: The individual is unable to perform at least two activities of daily living (ADLs) without assistance.

Residual disability: The individual is unable to perform some work functions and suffers an income loss as a result. Benefits are payable when the individual returns to work after a covered disability and suffers a loss of earnings due to the sickness or injury.

Preexisting Condition

The presence of an impairing condition that is not disclosed when applying for a policy is an obvious concern for an insurer who has not accounted for this increased risk. As such, many policies include language that denies benefits for such conditions. Application of this language in the administration of a policy can be complicated by whether a formal diagnosis had been made, whether a reasonable individual should have sought treatment, and the relationship of the undisclosed condition to the actual condition causing disability at the time that a claim occurs.

Attending Physician

In many policies the term "physician" is narrowly defined as an individual with a medical degree for the purposes of those permissible to attest to impairment in relation to an individual's claim of disability. However, for practical purposes, non-physician behavioral health specialists acting within the scope of their license are often acceptable as an "attending physician" for an insurer.

Medical Care Requirement

Most policies include language that indicates an individual must be receiving care for the claimed condition causing disability. Contractual language can vary significantly with respect to the specific requirements of this treatment, ranging from "under a doctor's care" to receiving "appropriate care" that meets a reasonable standard of care.

Examination

Most policies provide for the opportunity for the insurer to have a claimant independently examined. Specific policy language can vary significantly in this regard, with some allowing only for evaluation by a "physician" and others with broader language allowing for evaluation by the most appropriate health professional to the condition and impairment at hand. Multiple examinations may be completed over the course of any particular claim.

Independent Medical Evaluations

A review of the published literature with respect to forensic practice, as well as the references to neuropsychology within the legal arena, demonstrates an exponential growth of forensic practice over the last two decades (Kaufmann, 2009). While there are no specific published data on the increased use of neuropsychological IMEs within the realm of disability determination, personal experience has noted a gradual but steady increase in the use of neuropsychological assessment over the last decade. Much of this increase is based on the utility of neuropsychological techniques in determining functional impairment, addressing potential effort/motivation issues, and the ability of IME providers to appropriately and adequately address the underlying referral questions in these assessments. The utility of such assessments spans across not only psychiatric and neurological disorders, but also a variety of medical conditions for which the resulting functional impairment falls in the psychological and/or cognitive realm (Institute of Medicine, 2015).

Behavioral health specialists, including neuropsychologists, are increasingly recognized as essential for making determinations of impairments, limitations, and restrictions as they apply to behavioral health disability (these terms are further defined later). Such professionals are frequently called upon by private and public entities to provide evaluations and opinions to help understand some of the complex intra-individual and contextual issues involved with respect to the presence of potential work-related impairments. The goal of this section is to describe the context of disability-related evaluations.

At present, a thorough individual evaluation by a behavioral health specialist is considered to be the most comprehensive method for clarifying the often complex and multifactorial presentations of individuals reporting work-related impairments and/or disability secondary to behavioral health conditions. Private and public entities are growing in their understanding that the complexities discussed in this section related to understanding behavioral health impairments and/or disability underscore the need for an individualized assessment approach. The broad goal of such assessments is to examine, at an individual level, variables identified as being important clinical and contextual contributors to the experience of work-related impairment and/or disability (e.g., variables related to symptom constellations, symptom severity, motivation, work setting, economic circumstances, and job satisfaction).

In its most basic form, a behavioral health IME could be defined as follows: a behavioral health assessment conducted by a behavioral health specialist, not otherwise involved in the care or treatment of the individual, at the request of a third party that is not the behavioral health specialist's general employer (Baum, 2005). We employ in this chapter the conventional use of the term IME as it is employed in a variety of settings. Others might argue that an "independent medical evaluation" by its very terminology is limited to evaluations completed by physicians. As noted earlier, individuals deemed qualified to comment on work-related impairments may be defined by contractual language and/or statute or by the utility of the unique information that they offer, and the behavioral health specialist is encouraged to be aware of these issues in any particular case.

Although at first blush this definition appears fairly straightforward, within the broad nature of this definition emerge multiple foundational areas worthy of further discussion. These areas, presented in question form, are discussed in the following.

In What Context is the Behavioral Health IME Conducted?

Guidotti (2003) indicated that IMEs are gaining in importance as referral sources increasingly appreciate the advantages of opinions offered by professionals who are not involved in a patient's or claimant's care and that this process can improve adjudication of claims. As the foregoing suggests, IMEs are often performed within the context of an adjudication process and/or dispute resolution, typically associated with some aspect of employment- or work-related functionality. These processes are typically viewed by both the retaining party and the party undergoing a behavioral health IME as having very real financial (e.g., issues related to earning capacity, benefit amount, and/or settlement amount) and personal (e.g., questions of honesty, integrity, and accuracy) consequences. Moreover, an IME may be requested within the ongoing context of a formal legal dispute. As such, the conceptual issues and practical application of services associated with a behavioral health IME are best viewed within the context of a forensic evaluation (American Psychological Association, 2013; Anfang & Wall, 2006; Bush et al., 2005a). Vore (2007) observed that the critical reasoning associated with a behavioral health IME is most similar to that of forensic personal injury evaluations that involve highly specialized behavioral health knowledge, skills, and techniques.

Within a forensic context, there are multiple issues that the behavioral health specialist should consider prior to entering into an agreement to perform an IME. These evaluations require specialized knowledge, as well as specialized procedures that make them distinctly different from clinical evaluations. Guidotti (2003) offers a broad-based description of the basic differences between clinical and forensic behavioral health evaluations. These differences are characterized in relation to nine primary areas:

1. The professional role of the examiner as it differs from that of clinician and/or patient advocate;
2. A decreased emphasis on diagnosis;
3. The manner in which human behavior is conceptualized within the evaluation;
4. The nature of the work product that follows from the professional relationship;
5. The perceived level of trust/credibility in relation to the individual's responses;
6. The level of proof needed in support of the opinions that arise from the evaluation;
7. The temporal focus of the evaluation;
8. The level of professional and/or ethical accountability;
9. Accurate determination of which party is the client.

It is important that the behavioral health specialist providing an IME maintain familiarity with these issues, as they apply to the IME process. Familiarity with these issues gives rise to more thorough preparation and a form of critical thinking that serves to protect the objectivity of the evaluation and the reliability of resulting conclusions and opinions. Ignoring such issues places the IME process at risk.

Who are Potential Third Parties that May Request a Behavioral Health IME?

Plan Administrators

The referral source requesting a behavioral health IME often defines the type of IME to be performed. Evaluations that address the topic of disability or employment/work functionality have been described as falling within two broad categories: evaluations related to an individual's inability to work, and evaluations related to an individual's capacity to resume or to continue working (Anfang & Wall, 2006).

The first of these categories encompasses what many practitioners have come to know as the classic disability evaluation. This referral is typically initiated by a state Disability Determination Service, a private insurance company administering disability or workers' compensation insurance, or, more infrequently, an attorney representing a claimant. Referral questions associated with this category typically revolve around the degree of work/employment-related impairment associated with a potential behavioral health condition and/or a condition impacting on cognitive function.

Employers

The second category of IME is more typically associated with an individual's desire to maintain employment. For instance, an individual may seek work-related accommodations under the Americans with Disabilities Act (ADA) or may be contesting a work-related dismissal associated with a perceived behavioral health condition. Referral questions in this category may also relate to safety concerns in the workplace. Referrals in this category are typically initiated by an employer, a licensing board, or an attorney representing an individual's interests in association with these matters. These types of evaluations have also been referred to as "fitness for duty evaluations" and "return to work evaluations."

A fitness for duty (FFD) evaluation occurs within the employer–employee context. There are two general scenarios that lead an employer to request an FFD. The first is one in which an employee has been absent from work due to sickness or injury and in light of the nature of her occupation, concern is present regarding her capacity to resume her occupational duties without issue. The second type of scenario is one in which the employee's behavior has raised concern regarding his occupational competency.

Results of an FFD evaluation generally fall into one of four categories:

1. Employee can return or continue with full-time work without conditions.
2. Employee can return or continue work but must participate in some form of ongoing treatment as a condition.
3. An employee may not return to work or should cease working pending ongoing treatment to restore his or her functional capacity.
4. An employee is unable to return or should cease working and is determined to be unable to ever (even with treatment) resume his or her prior position.

There are obviously constraints in an employer's ability to request that employees demonstrate their work competency that are governed not only by state and federal law, but also possibly by either civil service policies or collective bargaining agreements. It is incumbent on the employer seeking an evaluation to be clear about the employer's rights and responsibilities in this regard; the competent neuropsychologist should be at least aware of these issues and seek additional information as appropriate.

Historically, the involvement of psychology in the FFD realm has largely been in the work of policing. Over time, though, these types of evaluations are increasingly being performed in other settings. One area of particular interest is in the area of other medical professionals, either in the context of cognitive issues in aging or disruptive workplace behavior. The Joint Commission on Accreditation of Hospital Organizations (or The Joint Commission) issued a Sentinel Event Alert in 2008, making clear their expectations regarding a hospital's responsibility to address intimidating and disruptive behaviors in the workplace (Joint Commission, 2008).

Among the most useful texts for an individual seeking more information regarding FFD evaluations is Rostow and Davis's (2004) *Handbook for Psychological Fitness-for-Duty Evaluations in Law Enforcement.*

Issues from both IME categories may commingle. Such an example might include finding, within the context of conducting a disability-related behavioral health IME on behalf of a private insurance company, that an insured is also involved in an administrative action with the employer, in association with perceived threatening behaviors in the workplace. In such situations, examiner role confusion becomes a distinct possibility, with overlapping employment issues and multiple definitions of disability involved. It is essential that evaluators faced with such situations try to maintain clear conceptual boundaries.

Conclusions

There are considerable areas of ambiguity and complexity that exist in relation to definitions of disability and how such definitions address behavioral health conditions. For instance, there are broad contextual differences in how basic concepts such as disability, impairment, and mental health conditions are operationalized from definition to definition. Such differences often stem from whether impairment and/or disability are being viewed from a clinical, administrative, contractual and/or legal, or research-related perspective. Differences also exist depending on whether definitions were drafted from a public policy perspective (e.g., SSDI, ADA) or from the perspective of a private entity (e.g., long-term disability, short-term disability, individual disability), with public policy definitions typically employing language that is more inclusive. Unfortunately, the majority of disability-related definitions offer little specific guidance for conceptualization and assessment of behavioral health issues. Additionally, legal and/or contractual definitions of disability may vary radically, depending upon the context in which a behavioral health IME is performed.

The typical behavioral health IME includes a thorough evaluation of clinical, motivational, and contextual (e.g., work setting) factors that contribute to an overall understanding of potential functional impairments. From a definitional standpoint, impairments are broadly viewed as functional difficulties caused by sickness or injury. Impairments essentially reduce functional capacity by two mechanisms: limitations (what a person cannot do) and restrictions (what a person should not do).

Unlike clinical practice, the realm of independent neuropsychological evaluations (referred to hereafter in the generic form—independent medical evaluations, or IME) and similar types of non-clinical evaluations is an area of professional practice for which most neuropsychologists have little to no training. While some neuropsychologists have been fortunate to have had some prior exposure to at least the rudimentary aspects of this type of evaluation during the course of their training, the vast majority of neuropsychologists are ill prepared to fully competently begin to offer this service (without consultation) at the time that they initially agree to participate in such an evaluation. Further, for the practitioner looking for guidance and standards of professional conduct in this arena, there are few comprehensive resources that address the range of issues raised by these types of evaluations or clear standards by which to assess their competence. The purpose of this book is to provide a primer (and/or refresher) to prepare one to conduct these types of assessments and to review the evolving literature that is coalescing into a standard of practice.

2

Ethical and Professional Considerations

Consistent ethical practice in the performance of independent neuropsychological evaluations does not occur by accident. A concerted effort is required to provide services that (a) are informative to decision-makers and facilitate just decisions, (b) avoid directly harming the parties involved, and (c) safeguard the tools, techniques, and reputation of the profession. Intent to attain a high standard of ethical practice is evident initially through demonstration of professional competence in clinical neuropsychology in general and as applied in the specific context of IMEs. Ethical competence is dependent upon (a) the knowledge and skills of clinical neuropsychology, (b) an awareness and understanding of ethical and professional guidelines and requirements, and (c) familiarity with common pitfalls and risks associated with suboptimal ethical conduct. Ethical competence is necessary for sustained successful performance of IMEs. Such ethical competence helps independent examiners anticipate and avoid ethical misconduct, and a structured and systematic approach to ethical decision-making can help examiners address ethical challenges when they are encountered (Bush, 2007; Bush, Connell, & Denney, 2006).

In this chapter we provide questions that independent neuropsychological examiners may encounter or may ask themselves, followed by sections of ethical and professional resources that can direct examiners to sound solutions. Although many resources exist to guide neuropsychologists, the primary resources referenced here include the American Psychological Association's

(APA) *Ethical Principles of Psychologists and Code of Conduct* (EPPCC; APA, 2010), *Standards for Educational and Psychological Testing* (SEPT; American Educational Research Association, American Psychological Association & National Council on Measurement in Education, 2014), *Specialty Guidelines for Forensic Psychology* (SGFP; APA, 2013), and position statements of other professional organizations, particularly the American Academy of Clinical Neuropsychology (AACN) and the National Academy of Neuropsychology (NAN).

This chapter presents questions that have ethical implications or that involve ethical challenges. First, the questions are provided; then, the relevant ethical standards (ES), principles, or guidelines are presented.

Professional Competence

How Do You Determine that Completing an IME Falls within Your Boundaries of Professional Competence?

To comply with EPPCC Ethical Standard (ES) 2.01 (Boundaries of Competence), you should be able to describe specific education, training, supervised experience, consultation, study, or professional experiences that serve as the basis for your competency. Board certification provides the clearest evidence of competence in neuropsychology, leaving board-certified neuropsychologists the task of citing how they learned to apply their neuropsychology knowledge and skills in the unique IME context. Because there are very few formal training programs in forensic neuropsychology (as an example of one, see Hoy-Watkins, Bush, & Sesta, in press), participation in IME continuing education workshops at professional conferences, self-study, and consultation with experienced colleagues help prepare neuropsychologists to competently perform IMEs. Given the complexity and evolving nature of the IME process, an ongoing program involving these same activities can help neuropsychologists maintain competence over time (ES 2.03, Maintaining Competence). The SGFP states, "To maintain the requisite knowledge and skill, forensic practitioners keep abreast of developments in the fields of psychology and the law" (Guideline 2.02, Gaining and Maintaining Competence; p. 9).

What Particular Aspects of Current Established Scientific and Professional Knowledge in Assessing Impairment Should One be Familiar with in the Context of IMEs (ES 2.04, Bases for Scientific and Professional Judgments)?

A number of informative texts on forensic neuropsychology are now available and provide information needed to supplement basic clinical neuropsychological literature (Bush, Demakis, & Rohling, in press; Heilbronner, 2005; Horton & Hartlage, 2010; Larrabee, 2011; Sherman & Brooks, 2012). The relatively few scholarly publications that specifically address neuropsychological IMEs are particularly relevant resources (Bush et al., 2005a; Bush & Heilbronner, 2012; Heilbronner & Bush, in press; Lovejoy & Oakes, 2012).

Is the Use of a Technician and/or Interpreter Appropriate in the Context of an IME? Are There Limits to Their Roles and, If So, How Do You Establish these Limits?

There are instances in which delegation of work to others (ES 2.05) is both necessary and appropriate. When delegating work in the context of neuropsychological IMEs, neuropsychologists take reasonable steps to delegate only those activities that the person is competent to perform given his or her education, training, and experience, and provide the level of supervision needed to ensure that the services are provided in a competent manner. Independent examiners strive to avoid promoting or allowing assessment by unqualified persons (ES 9.07), seeking those with appropriate training and experience. Position and educational statements by professional organizations present in more specific detail recommendations for effective and ethical use of non doctoral-level personnel (AACN, 1999; NAN, 2000b; Puente et al., 2006) and interpreters (Judd et al., 2009) in conducting neuropsychological evaluations.

Human Relations

Is it Ever Appropriate to Offer Treatment Recommendations Directly to a Claimant and/or Provide Other Professional Services Following an Evaluation?

Maintaining boundaries between the roles of independent examiner and treating doctor is important for the promotion of objectivity. Retaining parties often do not want their IME examiners to offer treatment recommendations, and some specifically request that no opinions about treatment be offered. In contrast, other retaining parties want to know whether an examinee can be expected to improve if provided additional or different treatment. In either case, examiners typically do not provide feedback about results or recommendations or other clinical services to examinees. To do so could introduce a dynamic that blurs the relationship between independent examiner and treating doctor and is thus potentially harmful to the integrity of the IME process (ES 3.05, Multiple Relationships; SGFP 4.02, Multiple Relationships). Examinees should be informed at the outset that they will not receive written or verbal feedback directly from the examiner (ES 9.10, Explaining Assessment Results). Exceptions exist if the independent examiner believes that the examinee is in imminent danger because of psychiatric or medical/neurological reasons, in which case the examiner's obligation is to promote the safety and well-being of the examinee by making recommendations or providing services (e.g., calling an ambulance) as needed. Additionally, in some IME contexts, it could be acceptable practice to inform the examinee that continued treatment is recommended. Conveying such information, if not opposed by the retaining party, could reduce the examinee's anxiety about his or her future care and may have no harmful effects on the IME process.

Does Becoming a Member of an IME Panel Raise Issues of a Conflict of Interest?

The professional and financial relationships and interests inherent in serving on a panel of professionals seeking IME work could raise questions about examiner objectivity and effectiveness, which could reflect a perceived or actual conflict of interest (ES 3.6). However, neuropsychologists have the same right as other businesses to promote and market their services, which can include serving on IME panels, advertising in legal publications, and direct outreach to other health-care professionals, attorneys, and IME vendors. In their publicity and marketing endeavors, neuropsychologists adhere to requirements for ethical practice (ES 5.01, Avoidance of False or Deceptive Statements), taking particular care to avoid misrepresenting credentials or presenting themselves as aligned with one side or the other in adversarial or adjudicative processes.

Do You Have Established Policies and Procedures to Clarify Your Role with the Both the Referring Party and the Claimant?

Neuropsychologists performing IMEs have obligations to both the retaining parties and examinees (ES 3.07, Third- Party Requests for Services; SGFP 4, Relationships; SGFP 4.01, Responsibilities to Retaining Parties), including responsibility to communicate the parameters of the examination and other relevant information to both parties (SGFP 6.02, Communication With Those Seeking to Retain a Forensic Practitioner; 6.03, Communication With Forensic Examinees). Maintaining policies and procedures that explain and clarify roles and other aspects of the independent examinations facilitates communication with all parties, reduces the potential for misunderstanding, and promotes a more positive experience for everyone involved.

Is it Appropriate to Contact a Treating Provider to Obtain Additional Information in the Course of Evaluation? If Not, Why Not? If So, What Information Do You Reveal or Not Reveal to the Provider?

Independent examiners, like clinicians, have a responsibility to communicate with other health-care professionals, including treating providers, when the information to be exchanged is important for the purpose for which the service is being provided. For example, in the course of an evaluation it may be helpful to clarify the content of records or the basis for a provider's opinion regarding specific aspects of the case. The examiner determines for each whether such communication is needed and, if so, the nature of the information to be requested and provided (ES 3.09, Cooperation with Other Professionals).

The SGFP (6.04, Communication With Collateral Sources of Information) states that the information conveyed by the examiner consists of that which will help the collateral source decide whether to participate. Such information includes "who has retained the forensic practitioner; the nature, purpose, and intended use of the examination or other procedure; the nature of and any limits on privacy, confidentiality, and privilege; and whether their participation is voluntary" (p. 13). Independent examiners take care not to share information that will bias the information provided by the collateral source or that will affect the validity of the examinee's responses or performance.

Do You Have a Specific Procedure for Informed Consent in the Context of an IME? Are You Prepared for a Claimant to be Unwilling to Sign Any Documents (On Advice of Their Attorney)?

"Because substantial rights, liberties, and properties are often at risk in forensic matters, and because the methods and procedures of forensic practitioners are complex and may not be accurately anticipated by the recipients of forensic services, forensic practitioners strive to inform service recipients about the nature and parameters of the services to be provided" (SGFP 6, Informed Consent, Notification, and Assent, p. 12; see also ES 3.10, Informed Consent, and ES 9.03, Informed Consent in Assessments). The nature of the information provided and the requirements for consent versus assent vary based on the type of independent examination being conducted and the cognitive capacity of the person being examined. Sample consent forms that document relevant issues to be covered during the informed consent process have been offered for forensic neuropsychological examinations (Bush et al., 2005a) and for neuropsychological IMEs specifically (Bush & Heilbronner, 2012).

Privacy and Confidentiality

Do You Allow Recording and/or Observation of Your Clinical Interview and/or Testing? If Not, Why Not? If So, How Do You Handle the Practical Issues of Recording and Chain of Custody?

Although differences exist across jurisdictions, examinees undergoing IMEs for Workers' Compensation commonly have a legal right to record and/or have third parties present during the examination. Such laws typically do not distinguish between medical and neuropsychological examinations, with the latter having a well-established evidence base revealing that the presence of third parties affects test performance (see, for example, the special issue of the *Journal of Forensic Neuropsychology* edited by McCaffrey, 2005, and the update by Howe & McCaffrey, 2010). Because of such effects, professional organizations have taken the position that, with few exceptions, involved third-party observers (e.g., attorneys or their representatives) should not be allowed during neuropsychological evaluations, including forensic evaluations (AACN, 2001; NAN, 2000a). Thus, because of the effects of observation, including recording devices, on examinee test performance and the threat to test security, observation and/or recording of neuropsychological testing should not be allowed. This position poses a bind between ethical and legal requirements, requiring the examiner to make known the ethical obligation and to take steps to resolve the matter in a manner consistent with professional ethics and guidelines (ES 1.02, Conflicts Between Ethics and Law, Regulations, or Other Governing Legal Authority).

Some independent examiners have argued that because (a) the law allows recording and/or observation of examinations and/or (b) if they do not perform the examination, someone else (perhaps less qualified) will do it anyway, they will conduct the examination with recording and/or observation. Such arguments reflect the sacrificing of ethical principles. Although the law allows recording and/or observation, we do not have to allow it. We can refuse to perform examinations under such constraints. More than a few times, examinee representatives have insisted on recording or observation, even after being educated about the drawbacks of such procedures and the stances of professional organizations, stating that "the neuropsychologist down the street allows it." The reply given has been, "Just because he is willing to practice in a manner that is inconsistent with professional guidelines and standards of practice does not mean that I am. Feel free to go down the street." Such decisions result in lost revenue but the maintenance of high standards of ethical practice.

In contrast to recording and observation of testing, recording or quiet and unobtrusive observation of the interview poses little risk of harm or impact on the validity of the information. In fact, recording could promote accuracy in examinee reporting of information. One risk is that the examinee or a representative may, intentionally or otherwise, edit the recording in a manner that misrepresents the exchange of information and misleads subsequent listeners. For that reason, examiners who permit recording of the interview should also make their own recording. Secretive recording of any part of the examination process by either party is deceitful and should not occur or be encouraged (Bush, Pimental, Ruff, Iverson, Barth, & Broshek, 2009). Consistent with the bioethical principle of respect for autonomy, neuropsychologists who plan to record first obtain permission from the examinees and/or their legal representatives (ES 4.03, Recording).

How Do You Balance What May or May Not be Relevant from a Claimant's History in the Context of an IME?

To help ensure that only relevant information is documented in reports, independent examiners maintain focus on the purpose of the examination and pursue and report information that is germane to the purpose of the examination (ES 4.04, Minimizing Intrusions on Privacy). Information that is not relevant to the goals of the examination is typically not pursued and, if obtained through records or report by the examinee or a collateral source, is not reported. Communication of sensitive personal information that is clearly irrelevant to the purpose of the examination, such as sexual orientation in a case in which that has no bearing, may be viewed as a violation of the examinee's privacy. However, in situations in which the examiner is uncertain about whether the information may be relevant, clinical judgment that is supported by reasons for or against inclusion of the information in the report is needed.

Independent examiners should be particularly cautious when an examinee requests to share information "off the record." In the context of neuropsychological IMEs, when the nature of the information that the examinee may communicate is unknown, it is typically good practice to inform the examinee that nothing said can be considered off the record. It can be helpful to inform the examinee that without knowing what will be said, there is no way for the examiner to know in advance whether the information will need to be included in the report, and to remind the examinee of the limits to confidentiality, as previously explained during the informed consent process.

Do You Inform Claimants of the Content of Confidential Information (Surveillance, Investigation Reports, Pharmacy Records, etc.) Forwarded by a Third Party?

It can be helpful for the independent examiner to determine prior to meeting with the examinee whether information obtained from records or surveillance video suggests discrepancies or raises other questions that would benefit from clarification by the examinee. If such discussion is deemed potentially valuable, the examiner can contact the retaining party prior to the exam to request permission to discuss the materials with the examinee (ES 4.05, Disclosures). If information comes up during the examination that seems inconsistent with information received from other sources, it may be possible for the examiner to attempt to reach the retaining party during a break to obtain permission to discuss the materials previously received. If time or circumstances do not permit contacting the retaining party for permission, examiners should use their interviewing skills to attempt to clarify the matter in question. To help avoid the need for specific permissions such as this for each case, it can be helpful for independent examiners to include with the other written parameters of the examination their policy on discussing the content of records and surveillance videos with examinees. The process for handling such information is thus clear to all parties at the outset of every IME; retaining parties that prefer that such information not be shared with the examinee can raise their concerns at that time, and through discussion an agreement can be reached, or the examination does not go forward.

Record-Keeping and Fees

Do You Document Your Evaluation in Such a Way that it can be Subjected to Peer Review (i.e., Tracking Order of Tests, Complete Scoring, Legible Notes)?

Neuropsychological IME reports are routinely reviewed by colleagues who strive, often with a critical eye, to understand the information, data, and reasoning that underlie the conclusions that were reached. To do so, the colleagues may attempt to replicate the process used by the IME examiner—a process that requires access to the information relied upon by the examiner. This process is facilitated by examiners who document thoroughly, clearly, and legibly, with the goal of cooperating with, rather than subverting, the peer review process (ES 3.09, Cooperation With Other Professionals; ES 6.01, Documentation of Professional and Scientific Work and Maintenance of Records).

Do You Have Specific Procedures for Sorting and Storing Claim Information (i.e., Copies of Treatment Records, Test Data, the Report)?
Whether in paper or electronic form or both, neuropsychological IMEs tend to involve, through records received and generated, a tremendous amount of information and materials. Although organizational and storage approaches may differ, examiners have a responsibility to maintain and facilitate access to the materials in a manner consistent with ethical and legal requirements and guidelines (ES 6.02, Maintenance, Dissemination, and Disposal of Confidential Records of Professional and Scientific Work). Additionally, ethical practice requires examiners to be aware the risks as well as the advantages of the different storage options (see Bush & Schatz, in press, for addition information).

Do You Have Clear Fee Practices in Writing?
Clarity regarding fees and financial arrangements promotes a rewarding professional experience for both the independent examiner and the retaining party. Most experienced independent examiners have a written fee schedule that describes, at a minimum, the fee amount, whether a flat or hourly fee, the timing of the payment (e.g., in advance or following completion of the report), and the "no show" or late cancellation time frames and fees. The compensation and billing arrangements should be agreed upon by the examiner and retaining party as early as feasible in the professional relationship (6.04, Fees and Financial Arrangements) and should be documented in writing to help avoid misunderstandings. The arrangements include discussion of what will occur if the actual fees exceed or will likely exceed the initially anticipated amount (SGFP 5.02, Fee Arrangements), such as if additional records are received that must be reviewed or if the examination could not be completed in the usual time frame.

Assessment

Do You Have An Assessment Process That is Comprehensive and Defensible to Address the Referral Questions and that Includes Tests that have Established Reliability and Validity for the Purposes for Which They are Being Used?

Independent examiners use multiple measures and procedures to obtain an understanding of examinees that satisfies the goals of the IMEs (ES 2.04, Bases for Scientific and Professional Judgments; ES 9.01, Bases for Assessments). Examiners combine qualitative aspects of assessment with empirically supported methods, with the purpose of arriving at conclusions that are accurate and defensible. Commonly used neuropsychological measures (e.g., Rabin, Barr, & Burton, 2005; Sweet, Meyer, Nelson, & Moberg, 2011) and procedures are typically appropriate for most IMEs (ES 9.02, Use of Assessments), although modifications or accommodations may be needed for examinees who have substantial sensory or motor deficits or other limitations that make standardized test administration inappropriate for understanding the construct of interest. When use of uncommon measures or departures from standardized administration procedures is indicated, examiners describe in their reports the changes that were made, the reasons for the changes, and the apparent effects on the conclusions. That neuropsychology is an evidence-based specialty makes it particularly appealing to administrative and judicial decision-makers.

As Part of the Informed Consent Process, Do You Inform Claimants of Your Intention to Measure Effort/Motivation?

Independent examiners provide examinees with information needed to make a decision about whether to participate in the IME, including the nature of the examination (ES 9.03, Informed Consent in Assessments; SEPT 8.2). SGFP 11.01 (Accuracy, Fairness, and Avoidance of Deception) states, in the context of public statements, reports, and testimony, that examiners do not engage in deception. In the context of research, ES 8.07 (Deception in Research) states that deception is not used unless the deception is justified by the importance of the outcome and there are no alternatives, and the deception is later explained to the deceived study participants as soon as possible.

In the case of neuropsychological assessment, deception by the examiner is a necessary and unavoidable aspect of the process. Symptom and performance validity measures are an essential aspect of neuropsychological evaluations (Bush et al., 2005b; Heilbronner et al., 2009). For such measures to be of value, examinees cannot know that, or how, they are measuring validity. Therefore, the examinees must be deceived in this way. SEPT Standard 8.2 states that although test takers are typically provided in advance enough information about a test to make an informed decision about whether to participate, "[e]xceptions occur when knowledge of the purposes or intended score uses would violate the integrity of the interpretations of the scores, such as when the test is intended to detect malingering" (p. 134). However, because neuropsychologists generally strive to promote accuracy and truthfulness in their professional activities (APA General Principle C, Integrity), it has been recommended that independent examinees be informed that their effort and honesty will be assessed, without describing how or at what points during the examination such assessment will occur (Bush, 2013; Bush & Heilbronner, 2012;). Such information does not invalidate the use of the validity measures and may result in some examinees who were planning to attempt to mislead the examiner deciding to approach the evaluation in a valid manner.

Do You Have the Flexibility to Adjust Your Assessment Procedures to Account for Age, Cultural, Language, Disability, or Other Differences that Might be Presented and Affect Assessment Results?

Many factors influence performance on neuropsychological tests, some of which do not reflect cerebral functioning and some of which are not accounted for by normative data sets, but that does not mean that neuropsychological measures are without value in such cases. Independent examiners use their educated judgment and understanding of the scholarly literature to obtain an understanding of the person, including the constructs of interest, that is as accurate as possible, noting how their conclusions have been limited by such characteristics (ES 9.06, Interpreting Assessment Results). To obtain such an understanding, examiners may need to use test modifications, trained interpreters, or other non-standardized methods or procedures. Although some deviations from usual procedures can be anticipated and prepared for in advance, the ability to adjust the approach to assessment in the moment can bring value to an otherwise fruitless endeavor.

Are You Using Older Tests When Newer Versions (and/or Normative Data) are Available?

How do you determine that a test is obsolete? The SEPT states that "[t]est takers have the right to be assessed with tests that meet current professional standards" (p. 131). The EPPCC (ES 9.08, Obsolete Tests and Outdated Test Results) requires practitioners to avoid using assessment measures that are obsolete or outdated for their current purpose. Some retaining parties and practitioners have taken these statements to mean that the newest version of a test should always be used. There has been a psychological urban legend that new versions of tests should be adopted within one year of their publication, but this position is baseless. For some patient populations, assessment contexts, and purposes, a new version of a test may be an immediate improvement over the previous versions, rendering the earlier version immediately obsolete. However, for more specialized purposes and for examinees not well represented in the test's normative data, the new test may not render the prior version obsolete for its current purpose. Bush (2010) concluded the following:

> Determining whether or when to transition to a new version of a test can be particularly difficult for clinicians in psychological specialties because it can take years after publication of a revised test for research with special patient populations to be performed and published. As a result, different clinicians may adopt newer versions of tests at different times or elect not to use the newest version, depending on the specific patient population and referral questions. Decisions regarding transitioning to new test revisions should be based on the scientific merits of the tests, not on an arbitrarily defined time frame. Clinicians ultimately must use their judgment regarding which test version is best for a given patient at a given point in time. (p. 7)

That being said, the burden may fall to the examiner to explain why an older version of a test was chosen for a specific examinee.

Are You Aware that Automated Test Scoring and/or Interpretation Services Offer Only Hypotheses and that the Interpretation Remains Your Responsibility?

Digital assessment applications, including computerized scoring and interpretation programs, provide an efficient, and now almost unavoidable for some tests, means of working with and understanding often extensive and complex data sets. Through advanced data analytics, informative diagnostic hypotheses and recommendations can be quickly generated. Despite their advantages, there are risks that the reports generated for a given patient may not accurately reflect the constructs of interest. Independent examiners retain responsibility for the results described and conclusions drawn in their reports and testimony, regardless of whether some or all of their conclusions were based on, or informed by, computer-generated reports (ES 9.09, Test Scoring and Interpretation Services).

Do Your Reports Provide a Clear Explanation of Test Results Such that the Referral Source Can Understand the Results?

Numerous hours of interviewing, testing, and reviewing records are of little value if the results and conclusions are not explained clearly and the referral questions addressed directly. Independent examiners strive to provide results to retaining parties in a clear and timely manner.

Can You Define the Difference Between the EPPCC Definition of Test Data (ES 9.04, Release of Test Data) and Test Material (ES 9.11, Maintaining Test Security), and Can You Satisfy Both Requirements? Do You Have Policies and Procedures to Provide Test Data with Test Security Being Maintained?

With *test materials* (ES 9.11) defined as "manuals, instruments, protocols, and test questions or stimuli," which should be safeguarded, and *test data* defined as "[t]hose portions of test materials that include client/patient responses," which should be released based on the client's consent unless doing so could cause substantial harm or misuse, practitioners cannot satisfy both ethical requirements. For some tests or subtests, such as a test of general fund of information that requires the examinee to provide very brief answers to factual questions, the data (i.e., examinee responses) can, with some effort, be separated from the test materials (i.e., questions). However, for other commonly used neuropsychological tests, such as list learning or figure copying tests, the data and stimuli are the same and cannot be separated, leaving the neuropsychologist in an ethical bind.

Much has been written on this topic since the requirement was drastically changed in the 2002 version of the EPPCC, including the publication of position statements by multiple professional organizations, including APA Division 40, the Association of Postdoctoral Programs in Clinical Neuropsychology, and AACN (Attix et al., 2007) and NAN (2003) (for more comprehensive reviews of this topic, see Bush & Martin, 2006; Bush, Rapp, & Ferber, 2010; Kaufmann, 2009). Most recently, the SEPT (Standard 6.7) clearly states, without the impractical attempt that exists in the EPPCC to parse out test materials from data, "Test users have the responsibility of protecting the security of test materials at all times" (p. 117). Many retaining parties request that raw test data be sent to qualified neuropsychologists whom they retain or employ, which is an ideal solution. Otherwise, the steps outlined by NAN (2003) serve as a sound model for addressing requests for raw test data and other testing materials.

Resolving Ethical Issues

What Do You Do If You Complete an Evaluation and Render an Opinion But Later Learn that Your Opinion was Misunderstood or Misinterpreted?

In such a situation, the independent neuropsychological examiner should contact the retaining party in an attempt to clarify the matter (ES 1.01, Misuse of Psychologists' Work). If the retaining party is not involved in the misuse and is not interested in pursuing the matter, the examiner should seek permission to address the matter with the offending party. If such permission is not granted, and given that the retaining party is the holder of privilege, there may be little that the examiner can do unless an opportunity to exchange information is presented in the future (Bush & Martin, 2010; SGFP 8, Privacy, Confidentiality, and Privilege).

Are Your Institutional Policies at Odds with the Context of an IME (i.e., Patient Registration, Standard Informed Consent Forms, HIPAA Notifications)? Does Conducting Such an Evaluation Place One's Employer at Risk?

Having institutional policies that are at odds with the requirements of an IME can place the independent examiner in a difficult position that requires the examiner to communicate with one or both parties to attempt to arrive at a mutually agreeable solution (ES 1.03, Conflicts Between Ethics and Organization Demands). Because different retaining parties often have different requirements for aspects of their IMEs, an independent examiner employed by an institution (versus private practice) may be limited in his or her IME work to consulting only with those retaining parties whose policies coincide with the institution or are more flexible with individual cases.

In the Scope of the Review of Medical Records, IME Providers can Become Aware of Unethical and/or Unprofessional Behavior of Colleagues. How do or Would You Handle these Issues? Can Reports of Ethical Violations be Used as a Tactic to Discredit Colleagues?

With the exception of extremely egregious misconduct, psychologists are generally advised to contact colleagues informally to address apparently unethical or unprofessional conduct (ES 1.05, Reporting Ethical Violations). However, in forensic work, because the retaining party holds the privilege, the examiner would need the retaining party's permission to contact the colleague, and retaining parties often do not support or allow such contact. There is a risk for the retaining party that such contact could be viewed as an attempt to intimidate, threaten, or otherwise unduly influence the other practitioner. Retaining parties also may lack an understanding of the importance of addressing a behavior that is readily apparent to the neuropsychologist as being inappropriate, particularly if it involves nuances of the specialty (e.g., use of inappropriate norms leading to inappropriate conclusions, misrepresentation of the results of validity assessment measures).

A more formal action to address the ethical misconduct, such as reporting an ethical violation to an ethics committee or licensing board or encouraging the retaining party to do so, while avoiding direct contact between colleagues, could also be viewed as a tactic to discredit the other practitioner. Additionally, some more ethically subtle actions that may seem like ethical misconduct to one practitioner may not rise to that level of seriousness to another, or the actions may reflect reasonable differences of opinion or practices among colleagues in a specialty in which considerable variability exists. To reduce the potential for frivolous ethics complaints, practitioners are advised to wait until the forensic matter at hand has been completely settled, which could take a number of years, and then, if the ethical issue still seems to need addressing, to take action at that time (AACN, 2003; Grote, Lewin, Sweet, & van Gorp, 2000). In the interim, the offending colleague's professional activities could have evolved, or he or she may no longer be engaged in clinical activities, or the intensity of the concern may have diminished with the resolution of the case. In contrast, for colleagues who are frequently on opposite sides of forensic cases, there may never be a time when they do not have at least one shared case at any given time, so, depending on the situation, action may need to be taken at some point. Of course, in the case of egregious ethical misconduct, such as behavior that has caused physical or psychological damage to an examinee, an immediate ethical and/or legal response would be indicated and necessary.

Conclusions

Sustained successful performance of neuropsychological IMEs requires ethical competence. Understanding the differences between clinical evaluations and IMEs helps neuropsychologists anticipate, avoid, and address ethical challenges. This chapter has provided a small sample of common ethical challenges encountered with neuropsychological IMEs, but experienced colleagues, scholarly publications, and continuing education can help practitioners identify and manage additional challenges. Numerous resources exist to facilitate the ethical decision-making process, and use of a multi-resource approach in the context of a structured decision-making model (Bush, Connell, & Denney, 2006) can help position practitioners to provide a valuable service for administrative and judicial decision-makers.

3

Business Aspects of Performing Independent Medical Evaluations

Obtaining competence in the practice of IMEs begins with an understanding of relevant ethical and professional issues and a blending of these issues with the neuropsychologist's baseline level of competence in clinical practice. For many neuropsychologists, entering into the practice of IMEs represents their first foray outside of the health insurance payee realm of practice. There are several critical elements to consider

The Curriculum Vitae: Gateway to the Referral Source

The curriculum vitae (CV) is generally the first introduction of one's practice to potential referral sources and should accurately and appropriately reflect the professional experience you would bring to bear in the context of an IME. A practitioner's CV should provide sufficient information to demonstrate that he or she is professionally competent, knowledgeable of the condition in question, independent, and would reasonably be considered an "expert" by an administrative or judicial body.

There are several elements that make for a good CV. It should be neat and legible, should be up to date, and should provide sufficient information with respect to one's clinical, research, and other professional activities to provide a clear indication of one's professional experience. Licensure status should be explicitly noted. The indication of board certification is one of the most direct methods of asserting one's clinical competence. However, inclusion of vanity board certifications and/or other aggrandizements that attempt to mislead consumers with respect to competence should be avoided. "Vanity" boards are in effect a dissimulation of a peer review process and can be perceived as being worse than no board certification at all. Specialty boards that have a reasonably rigorous peer review process are typically appropriate.

A potential IME provider should understand that his or her CV may be liberally distributed in the public realm. As such, it is important to date one's CV, to provide it in pdf or other format that does allow for edits by others, and to not include irrelevant or overly personal information (e.g., height/weight, children's names, or private contact information) that you would not like to have in the public domain.

Identifying Referral Sources

IME referrals with respect to disability claims generally come from two sources: "vendors" and "brokers." An IME "broker" refers to business entities that connect potential IME providers directly to disability carriers. The role of the "broker" is to accumulate and vet providers for potential use by a carrier. Such vetting includes verifying licensure, malpractice status, availability to conduct evaluations, and specific areas of expertise. The broker often provides only a copy of an individual's CV and fee schedule for consideration by the carrier and may or may not participate in the actual scheduling of the evaluation. Brokers are most often compensated solely for having connected the carrier to the provider.

IME "vendors," on the other hand, are business entities that have their own panel of providers and manage an IME referral from a carrier within their own network. The carrier may have no say in the specific provider used for the evaluation. Vendors usually offer, as part of their service, a quality assurance component to the IME process by reviewing IME reports prior to their submission to the carrier. Such a review can be very helpful to the carrier by ensuring that referral questions are responded to, that there are no factual or administrative errors in the report, and that substandard providers are eliminated from the pool of potential providers. Vendor services often make use of a flat fee for an evaluation, and the vendor is compensated by the difference between the amount the carrier pays for the evaluation and the amount of compensation to the actual provider of the IME.

As a potential IME provider, entering into a contractual relationship with a vendor offers both pros and cons for a neuropsychologist. On the positive side, such a relationship can result in increased referrals, as well as mentoring and peer review services. These benefits are particularly helpful as one begins to provide IME services. On the negative side, the neuropsychologist's fees may be reduced in this type of relationship, the peer review process may be perceived adversely, and such relationships may have noncompete clauses that limit one's ability to seek any similar work on one's own. Participants in any vendor-related practice are cautioned to clarify the roles of any individuals involved in the IME process (e.g., suggested versus required aspects of the assessment), record-keeping by the vendor (e.g., drafts of reports, copies of test data, basis for them to release this information and to whom), and the standing of the vendor service in the marketplace (which has a high turnover).

Fees and Contracts

It is appropriate to generate a schedule of fees for professional activities that include IME-related services (record review, testing, interview, report writing) (see Appendix A). While some practitioners charge fees based on an hourly rate, some providers opt to indicate a flat fee for conducting an IME (with some flexibility if there are excessive records to review). Some providers may opt to provide both types of evaluation fee schedules, depending on the preference of the referring party. While there are some benefits of this "flat fee" arrangement for referral sources in terms of known fixed costs, in the case of evaluations that may require multiple visits such a system can become problematic, as the number of hours worked on a case increases for the provider. Providers do not want to put themselves in a position to argue that further testing did not occur due to limited fees. For this reason, the use of an hourly rate combined with an upfront estimate of hours for a "usual" IME is the more common practice. It would also be appropriate, in cases in which the "usual" number of hours is expected to be exceeded, to notify the referral source of the status of the evaluation. Any cancellation fees and/or administrative costs (copying, mailing, etc.) should also be clearly identified in one's fee agreement. It is important for the neuropsychologist to emphasize that compensation is based solely on his or her professional time, not on the outcome of the case.

Understanding the Purpose of the Referral

Disability carriers most often, but not always, make use of consulting neuropsychologists to assist with formulating the referral questions and requirements for an evaluation. This arrangement is often reduced to a generic referral letter but may be modified to address specific issues in a particular case. As such, an IME provider may be presented with requests and/or specific referral questions that are vague or unclear, or that fall outside his or her scope of expertise. It is important that IME providers review a referral letter in its entirety immediately upon receipt from a carrier to ensure that the referral is appropriate and to address any concerns immediately. A review of the information (records, disability forms, etc.) provided by the carrier well in advance of the actual assessment is also important for determining whether a conflict of interest may exist (e.g., the claimant is known to the provider through treatment or contact in the community, or close relationship with the claimant's treatment provider).

The Referral Letter

The following are examples of information contained in a typical referral letter from an individual disability insurer for the purposes of conducting an IME.

> Please do not comment specifically about whether the claimant is "disabled." Disability status is based on the claimant's contract and needs to be determined by insurance professionals. Your role is to form an independent opinion regarding the presence and degree of a claimant's impairment and any resulting restrictions (things they should not do) and limitations (things they are unable to do).

This section addresses the scope of the opinion being requested. The definitional concept of "disability" differs across settings. Because "disability" typically represents a contractual or legal concept, the neuropsychologist rarely makes this determination in the context of an IME. Instead, the neuropsychologist serves as a source of information for those seeking to determine "disability." While the neuropsychologist IME provider is not the arbiter of an individual's "disability" status, it is often helpful for the provider to be cognizant of the context in which the evaluation is being employed. For example, private disability insurance may employ definitions of disability that reflect an inability to perform the primary duties of one's occupation because of an injury or sickness (own occupation policy), or total disability may be defined as the inability to perform the primary duties associated with any occupation for which the individual is qualified by education, training, and/or experience (any occupation policy). A multitude of additional definitions of disability also exist, as well as specific contractual provisions.

Another section of the letter may state the following:

> We are interested in obtaining information about the claimant's current functioning based on standardized objective assessment and clinical interview rather than solely based on self-report. Because of this, we are not asking you for an opinion based only on the medical records and/or the claimant's self-report, though this provides the context for their current presentation.

This section makes clear that the psychometric testing results are perceived to be paramount in the identification of work-related impairments, rather than the claimant's self-report of such impairment. This is to clearly distinguish what might constitute a psychiatric IME, which includes only a clinical interview, mental status testing, and record review from the more comprehensive assessment of a neuropsychological IME.

Such letters commonly also state the following.

> Although a psychometrician can be used to administer certain tests, we ask that the primary psychologist conduct the clinical interview, select the tests to be administered, interpret the test data, and write the actual report.

While neuropsychologists (in most states) have the statutory right to make use of technicians and it is a standard of clinical practice to do so, it is important to make clear what aspects of the evaluation can be appropriately delegated to a technician and to note that the neuropsychologist remains responsible for the evaluation in its entirety. IME providers should be cognizant that the use of a technician in neuropsychological evaluations may come as an unwelcome surprise to claimants who have assumed they would be solely assessed by the neuropsychologist and who may perceive themselves as having been short-changed. Further, psychometricians may be less equipped and/or prepared to work with claimants who perceive the assessment process as adversarial. Defining the role of any technician to be used in the course of an evaluation should be covered in the initial informed consent procedure with the claimant.

Such letters often request the use of specific tests, as illustrated by the following:

> Please administer the MMPI-2 or MMPI-2-RF as part of the present evaluation. If indicated, the choice of neuropsychological battery remains your responsibility. However, we recommend that such evaluation include at least the following: the WAIS-IV, the WMS-IV, the Halstead-Reitan Neuropsychological Battery, and appropriate validity testing. Please include at least two assessments of effort or motivation (e.g., Word Memory Test, VIP, TOMM, and Victoria Symptom Validity). Please also complete any appropriate reviews of internal consistency or embedded validity indicators.

The proposed scope of testing to be included as part of an evaluation is only a suggestion to illustrate the comprehensive scope of the type of assessment being requested. It should be clear that what is being requested is (a) an objective assessment of cognitive and psychological functioning rather than reliance on self-report, (b) avoidance of obsolete or outdated tests, and (c) adequate and quantitative assessment of effort and honesty in the assessment process. Neuropsychologists should also be cognizant that at times the disability carrier may want to limit the scope of assessment procedures. Again, a careful review of the referral letter well in advance of the actual IME date will help to identify these types of issues and will allow time for discussion and understanding between both parties. It should also be noted that the use of a test for the first time in the context of an IME is ill-advised. The neuropsychologist should be adequately familiar and competent in the administration, scoring, and interpretation of any test employed in the assessment.

Neuropsychologists performing IMEs should expect to have their raw data requested and should be prepared to copy and send the materials to a qualified colleague appointed by the carrier and potentially to other colleagues if the claim is disputed. The referral letter is likely to include information similar to the following:

> A copy of all raw data should accompany your report. Please obtain the necessary authorization to send this data. Please send all raw data directly to our consulting neuropsychologist. Please

> mark the envelope to indicate that raw test data are included. This data will then be reviewed by the above-named consulting neuropsychologist and not included in the insured's claim file. Our consultant will subsequently destroy these copies. It is your responsibility to maintain a copy of all test data and relevant materials consistent with national guidelines and your local standards for psychological test materials.

This section provides notice that your report will likely be subjected to peer review that will include auditing of your test data and careful review of your report. The individual completing the peer review will often be identified to facilitate the transfer of test data. Note that issues of release of test data to individuals not qualified to interpret the information, as well as test security, are proactively addressed in this scenario. If these issues are not appropriately addressed (i.e., copies of the data are requested to be sent to a consulting nurse or psychiatrist), it is incumbent on the IME provider to make known the ethical and professional obligations in this regard prior to beginning the evaluation.

Some IME providers make use of colored paper for copies of test data that they provide to others. This technique limits the ability to make any further copies of the data and can serve to identify the individual to whom the data was initially forwarded. Further, a cover letter that accompanies copies of test data, reminding a fellow psychologist of his or her ethical obligations, can also be helpful.

Issues regarding feedback, dissemination of results, and treatment are also commonly covered in the referral letter, along the lines of the following paragraph:

> Please do not share the conclusions or results of this exam with the claimant. We may decide to share it with the claimant's provider who may in turn share the results with the claimant. Please indicate if you have any concerns in this area. Please note that we are not authorizing you to offer any direct treatment services to the claimant. Any correspondence and/or requests for information regarding this evaluation from any other entity should be directed to the disability carrier. Apart from your clinical staff, we do not authorize any individual to be present with the claimant during the interview or during the testing; nor do we give permission to have the testing process recorded in audio or video formats.

A number of critical elements of an IME are included in this paragraph. First, there is the reminder that the disability carrier is your client, and any sharing of the report you generate is the carrier's prerogative. Not all insurers share copies of IME reports with claimants, their providers, and/or their attorneys. It is also explicitly noted that you do not have the privilege to release your report (or data) in the absence of consent from the disability carrier. A neuropsychologist newer to the IME process should be cognizant of any conflicts between these conditions and their state statutes, and/or those of their employer.

The presence of third parties during a neuropsychological evaluation has been clearly demonstrated to have an effect on the results obtained, and there are several emphatic professional consensus papers on this issue (see Chapter 7 for a more detailed discussion of this topic). While you may consent to the presence of third parties in your clinical practice, your IME client may not agree to this. There are differing opinions with respect to the impact of a third party solely during the course of a clinical interview, particularly with respect to the relationship of the third party to the claimant (i.e., spouse/significant other, attorney, retained witness solely for this purpose). In the absence of a specific request from a disability carrier, neuropsychologists may establish their own policies and procedures in this regard, based on the research and practice guidelines.

Consistent with professional ethics, the neuropsychological IME report should accurately summarize the totality of the information obtained and upon which one's conclusions are based. The referral source is likely to specify questions to be addressed in the report. The following is an example of specific questions to be addressed in the report:

1. Is there evidence to suggest that symptom exaggeration or feigning was present during the evaluation? Is there evidence to suggest that the claimant was malingering? (If so, please integrate this information throughout your responses to these questions.)
2. Does the available information indicate the presence of non-clinical factors (i.e., legal, career dissatisfaction, economic factors, choice, lack of motivation for his/her profession) that play a role in the claim

of disability? If so, please indicate any significance of these factors in the claimant's reported inability to perform his/her occupation.

3. Is the claimant experiencing valid cognitive symptomatology that would result in occupational impairment (see enclosed occupational description) in completing his/her predisability duties? If so, please indicate any resulting specific occupational restrictions (things he/she should not do) or limitations (things he/she is unable to do) as well as the basis for each.
4. Do the evaluation results substantiate the presence of psychiatric and/or interpersonal skills impairment? If so, please indicate any resulting specific occupational restrictions (things he/she should not do) or limitations (things he/she is unable to do) as well as the basis for each.
5. Additionally, if the claimant is experiencing occupational impairment, is there evidence to suggest he/she could perform occupational duties with appropriate accommodations?
6. Based on your understanding of the basis for any current impairment, has the claimant reached maximum medical improvement?
7. Is the current treatment adequate?

These referral questions address the heart of the referral request, which is a description of the claimant's current functional status. In light of the base rate of poor effort and/or malingering in the context of disability claims (Chafetz & Underhill, 2013; Larrabee, 2005; Richman et al., 2006), it is critical to thoroughly consider such issues throughout the course of an IME.

Some clinicians consider the diagnosis of "malingering" to be controversial in the context of IMEs as a result of the poor operational definition of "malingering" in the *Diagnostic and Statistical Manual of Mental Disorders* (5th edition; *DSM-V*), the gray zone between poor effort (which may result from multiple causes) and intentional poor performance, and the limited contact of the IME provider with the claimant. Further, the overwhelming pejorative nature of a malingering "diagnosis" leaves many providers reluctant to make use of the term. More commonly, neuropsychologist IME providers have adopted the Slick et al. (1999) criteria for describing the probability of malingering of a neurocognitive disorder, rather than the broader use of the term (see update by Slick & Sherman, 2013). Further, the question of valid impairment (#3 in the list provided) presumes no problems with effort throughout the evaluation, in order to produce results that demonstrate a clear functional impairment. As such, a determination of the basis for any poor effort (irrespective of the etiology) is not necessarily needed to conclude the absence of the ability to establish valid impairment.

Review of Information from the Referral Source

Disability insurance carriers vary with respect to the types of information given to IME providers. While most carriers will at least provide copies of treatment records from relevant treatment providers, there are often additional sources of information in the claim file that may or may not be provided. If potentially valuable information seems to be missing from the records received, it is reasonable for an IME provider to request additional or updated records from the disability carrier (who will in turn obtain these records if possible).

Regarding treatment records, unfortunately they are too frequently barely legible, or of such poor quality that they provide little useful information regarding the claimant's symptoms and treatment over time, and fall well below psychological record-keeping standards (APA, 2007). Additionally, many mental health providers have both erroneous understanding of the Health Insurance Portability and Accountability Act (HIPAA) and the rights of their patients with respect to their medical records. When treatment records are requested from therapists, many assert the "psychotherapy notes" provision of HIPAA, with no actual understanding of what this provision allows. As such, few providers actually maintain a distinct "psychotherapy notes" section of their medical records, and they fail to maintain a concurrent treatment record that includes the required documentation of treatment visits, ongoing symptoms, treatment plan, and so on. Further, some therapists also invoke a privilege to not provide records in the face of a valid authorization from their patient. However, in most states, this privilege is very limited and applies only to the release of records directly to the patient. Nonetheless, disability carriers will frequently settle on receiving a narrative report from a treatment provider when records are not provided. Some carriers may request a specific format to the narrative, whereas others may not.

Consent Forms

It is encouraged that the neuropsychologist develop specific consent forms for the purpose of completing an IME (advice of counsel and/or your malpractice carrier can be helpful in this regard; see Bennett et al., 2006). Such forms should not be overly general and should make clear the referral source, limits of confidentiality, and other aspects of the IME (Bush et al., 2005a; Johnson-Green et al., 1997). See Appendix B for an example of such consent (based on a variety of sources).

Whenever possible, the signing of the consent form should be witnessed by an individual other than the neuropsychologist conducting the evaluation. Many claimants are instructed by their counsel to not sign any documents in the course of an evaluation that have not already been reviewed by counsel. In these cases, it would be appropriate to obtain a verbal consent from the claimant and to document this on the standard consent form. A copy of the form can then be provided to the claimant to be reviewed by his or her counsel at a later time.

Given the potential stakes for claimants, it is not unusual for them to have conducted some Internet-based search of the neuropsychologist provider and his or her practice prior to the evaluation. The neuropsychologist provider should be prepared for questions regarding his or her professional experience and practice patterns by claimants. Awareness of one's Internet presence and sensitivity to the claimant's perspective can improve the quality of the claimant–examiner interaction.

The Power of Rapport

A comprehensive, valid, and useful IME cannot be obtained without the full cooperation and effort of the examinee, yet many IME providers fail to take the time and effort to fully understand the context of the evaluation from the perspective of the examinee and/or to take the steps needed to ensure that the evaluation goes as smoothly as possible and to obtain a truly accurate understanding of the individual presenting to them.

Irrespective of the accuracy of the examinee's perspective of the rationale for an evaluation having been requested and/or the purpose of the evaluation, an IME provider should at least have empathy for the thoughts and feelings of the examinee. It is very common for examinees to present for the evaluation with these core beliefs: (1) the disability company believes I am malingering; (2) this process is a sham to deny me my benefits; (3) the IME provider is not objective and is on the side of the insurer; (4) the IME process ignores the opinions and treatment of my own health-care providers.

An IME provider should be prepared to accurately address concerns regarding the IME process as part of his or her efforts to establish rapport. Ideally, an IME examiner is not defensive regarding the preceding concerns, but rather is able to provide a neutral response that acknowledges a claimant's concern and that results in optimal effort and engagement in the evaluation process to yield reliable and valid results.

Conclusions

Entering into the realm of providing independent evaluations should be undertaken with careful consideration of the legal, ethical, and practical issues that might arise. IME providers should be aware of the need for specific authorizations, consent, and billing/contractual processes that arise in these types of evaluations. Further, in light of the significantly different nature of an IME evaluation from routine clinical evaluations, IME providers should make themselves aware of the scope of such evaluations and should make a thoughtful appraisal of their competence to complete the evaluation being requested, as well as taking steps to proactively prepare themselves for the administrative components of such evaluations.

4

Review of Records and Other Materials

The independent medical evaluation (IME) typically includes a review of a potential range of materials sent by an insurance carrier or a representative of the insurance carrier such as an IME vendor. These materials may be sent to the IME provider/examiner under a single cover or in multiple mailings over time. With regard to timing, it can be advantageous for the examiner to review the IME-related materials before initiation of the actual face-to-face examination. As discussed in the following, familiarity with the background information can aid with regard to neuropsychological and psychological test selection, as well as formulation of pertinent interview questions.

The IME provider/examiner is often in a unique position with regard to the examination of an insured. That is, the IME provider may be given access to more sources of information than the insured's own attending physician or clinical provider. This allows for a more expansive view of medical and functional information related to the insured's reported impairments and work-related restrictions and limitations.

It is worth noting that there may be instances in which the examiner is asked only to review a set of records and to provide specific opinions, or to answer specific questions based on the available clinical information from a disability claim file. These are sometimes referred to as "Paper IMEs." Such circumstances might occur when an insured refuses to attend a face-to-face IME, an attorney representing an insured advises him or her not to attend a scheduled face-to-face IME, or when a claims examiner is simply seeking an independent external expert opinion as to the support that a set of records provides related to claimed work-related impairments, limitations, and restrictions.

From the standpoint of timing, if it is possible, it is often advantageous to conduct an initial review of the IME-related materials prior to the face-to-face examination of an insured. An initial review of the IME-related materials is advantageous on multiple levels. For instance, it allows the examiner to become familiar with the medical or behavioral health condition at hand and the claimed impairments, limitations, and restrictions that may be associated with the claimed condition. An initial review of the materials also allows an examiner to engage in a self-evaluation as to whether he or she feels qualified to evaluate the condition and its associated work-related impairments, limitations, and restrictions. Finally, an initial review of the materials gives the examiner time to contact the referral source about any clarifications that are necessary regarding the IME records, the IME questions, or the structure of the evaluation.

The materials received by an examiner in preparation for an IME may be somewhat scant or they may be voluminous. If the examiner feels that there may be records or documents that he or she does not have that would be useful in developing opinions related to the IME referral questions, it is appropriate to contact the referral source to ask about the possibility of obtaining such documents.

The IME materials sent to an examiner may include a range of documents that are part of a disability claim file. It is important to note that separate carriers may have differing policies or opinions as to which claim file documents are appropriate to send as part of an IME. For instance, depending on the type of insurance carrier, it may be commonplace for companies to employ behavioral health specialists to review disability claim file materials and to provide opinions about whether or not the available information within the file supports the insured's claimed impairments, restrictions, and limitations (Lovejoy & Oakes, 2012; Piechowski, 2006). Carriers may have different views with regard to sending these internal reviews as part of the IME materials. Some companies feel that this form of review offers important insights as to the evolving clinical impression of an insured's claimed disability. As such, companies such as these typically send their internal behavioral health/neuropsychological reviews as part of the IME materials. Companies such as these view an IME provider as capable of integrating these reviews in an unbiased fashion, along with numerous other opinions and data points contained within the IME materials. Other carriers may view their internal reviews as potentially biasing to an IME provider given that the opinions were rendered by colleagues who share similar credentials within the field. As a result, companies such as these will typically withhold their internal reviews and will not include them with the IME materials.

As mentioned earlier, each referral source may differ significantly in terms of the volume and type of materials sent to an IME provider. With that said, IME materials may contain a mixture the following documents: an IME letter from the referral source; an attending physician statement (APS); a description of the claimed disability from the insured; documentation of conversations between the claims examiner and the insured; field visit reports; internal vocational rehabilitation reviews; previous IMEs; medical and/or mental health records; internal medical and/or behavioral health reviews; attending physician telephone calls; and social media searches and video surveillance. Comment about each of these documents will be offered in the following sections, in terms of their relevance to understanding an insured's claimed work-related impairments, restrictions, and limitations.

The IME Letter

This typically serves as an introduction letter to the examiner performing an IME. This letter often includes a brief summary of the claim and information about the insured. Attempts are often made to reference different documents within the claim file, in an unbiased and fact-based fashion, that relate to the insured's condition, impairments, limitations, and restrictions. The summary within the letter may also convey the reasons that a carrier is requesting an IME, in relation to an insured's reported work-related impairments, restrictions, and limitations.

The IME letter may also reference specific requests from the insurance carrier. These requests may relate to how the evaluation is structured in terms of test selection, how the evaluation is structured in terms of the time frame in which an insured is evaluated (e.g., over a single day, over multiple days), how a carrier prefers an examiner to respond to a request for third-party observers, and how a carrier prefers that the raw data associated with the evaluation are handled. For instance, carriers may request that the raw test data be copied and forwarded to them for later review by an internal behavioral health consultant. The letter will often include the credentials of an internal consultant/reviewer to help in alleviating any concerns about ethical obligations and sharing of raw psychological or neuropsychological test data. Finally, the IME letter will typically include any specific questions for the IME provider. Specifics regarding the typical questions associated with IMEs and the structure of an independent neuropsychological evaluation are covered in greater detail in Chapter 5.

Attending Physician Statement

Many disability carriers use a standard form to collect information about an insured's medical or behavioral health condition from their treating physician. This form is typically designed to collect information about an insured's symptoms, diagnosis, and medical or behavioral health treatment from a clinical provider. These forms also typically collect written information related to the treating clinician's view of how the insured's symptoms or conditions have resulted in work-related impairments, limitations, and associated clinician-imposed restrictions. These forms are often designed to give a fairly comprehensive view of the reasons a treating clinician views his or her patient as unable to perform some or all of the patient's work-related duties. The forms are also useful in that they often document many aspects of treatment and symptom presentation. Views related to prognosis and potential return to work dates may also be offered as part of this document.

Claimant Forms: An Insured's Description of His or Her Functional Impairments, Restrictions, and Limitations

Some carriers may send forms that are completed by an insured related to his or her own perception of work-related impairments, limitations, and restrictions. Some of these forms may also contain descriptions offered by an insured about his or her daily functioning. These forms typically document the insured's perceived ability to complete various daily functional tasks such as driving, doing household chores, socializing with others, paying bills, engaging in strenuous physical activities, and so on.

Telephone Call Summaries

Telephone contacts with an insured may be commonplace with an insurance carrier. These telephone calls are often memorialized as they contain information offered by an insured related to his or her work-related impairments, restrictions, and limitations. These conversations may be highly detailed, in terms of capturing a comprehensive description of the insured's condition, symptoms, associated functional impairments, functional capacity outside of work, daily activities, information about his or her occupation, job, relationships at work, and so forth. Other conversations may be narrower in focus, addressing specific issues or concerns raised by a carrier with an insured.

Field Visit Reports

Insurance carriers will sometimes send a representative for a face-to-face interview with an insured. The reports generated from these meetings often cover a range of topics, including clinical aspects of the insured's presentation, discussions about his or her impairments and functional limitations, and descriptions of how the insured presented in a face-to-face meeting. Observations regarding psychiatric symptoms, medical symptoms, and behaviors are often present in these reports. Information related to the insured's environment (if the interview was conducted at the insured's home) can also be found within these reports. Discussions that focus on occupational or job-related information can be addressed within these reports. In sum, these reports sometimes document face-to-face observations and more extensive interviews that may not be captured from documentation of telephone call contacts with an insured.

Vocational Rehabilitation Reviews

Carriers often employ or consult with vocational rehabilitation professionals. These professionals provide information that is important in understanding an insured's occupation. For instance, they may provide independent verification of an insured's occupation at the time of disability and of the functional requirements for his or her job or occupation. This document may include an analysis of the main duties that are part of an insured's occupation. It may include information as to how an insured describes her day-to-day job-related tasks and why it is that she currently believes that she cannot perform these tasks or duties. This document may also include comparisons of occupations if the insured is employed in a different occupation at the time of the evaluation. Such comparisons may include areas of overlap in abilities required to function within either occupation, as well as any differences in abilities required for either occupation. These documents may also include information about the insured's productivity at work, through an analysis of business calendars or schedules, billable work, Current Procedural Terminology (CPT) codes, and so on.

Previous IMEs

The records for review may also include past IMEs. These evaluations may be in the area of neuropsychology, psychology, or other medical specialties. These documents often provide useful information about functional deficits that may be associated with comorbid medical conditions. If the evaluation is in the area of neuropsychology or clinical psychology, the evaluations may contain important baseline information such as test scores or self-reports. These documents provide insight into the opinions of other experts who have evaluated the insured in the past.

Medical and/or Mental Health Records

These documents provide insight into the insured's treatment. The treatment may relate to the claimed impairments at hand, or the records may relate to treatment for co-occurring conditions that may or may not contribute to the claimed impairments, limitations, and restrictions. Some treatment records may make reference to an insured's work-related difficulties, while others may remain silent on the issue. Treatment records may provide insight into an insured's premorbid clinical functioning as well. For instance, an insured may have struggled with symptoms of depression, while maintaining adequate work-related functionality, before claiming a disability that is related to an exacerbation of his depression. Treatment records may also be an important source of behavioral observations related to the perceived presence or lack of presence for cognitive difficulties, emotional distress, pain related behaviors, and so on.

Internal Medical and/or Behavioral Health File Reviews

Carriers may employ physicians, psychologists, or neuropsychologists as consultants. These documents often contain a consultant's review of available records as well as his or her opinion as to whether the available information supports the insured's claimed work-related impairments, limitations, and restrictions. Carriers may differ as to whether these documents are provided as part of the record set sent to an IME provider.

Attending Physician Telephone Calls

These documents memorialize collateral contacts with an insured's treating clinicians. It is not uncommon for the consultants employed by a carrier to communicate with an insured's treatment providers, especially when the presence of a work-related impairment, limitation, or restriction appears unsupported or unclear. These documents often provide further information about the basis for a treatment provider's opinions about work-related impairment, limitations, or restrictions.

Social Media Searches and/or Video Surveillance

A disability claim file may also include direct insight into an insured's daily social activities and/or functional capacity. Information gleaned from publicly available social media sites may be provided as part of a set of records. These documents may provide insight into the insured's social activities, athletic activities, or work-related activities. Such information may be useful in understanding an insured's level and type of activity, particularly as it relates to areas of claimed impairment. Video surveillance may also be provided in a set of records. This may include a single day of surveillance or multiple days of surveillance. Again, data from these documents may provide direct insight into an insured's level of activity as well as the type and quality of activity he or she is able to perform. Such information may provide a useful comparison in relation to an insured's report of his or her own daily functional limitations.

Conclusions

The records and other materials that one might receive as part of an IME can be important sources of information for the IME provider. Although the background materials sent with each IME may differ on a case by case basis, understanding the type of information that each of these sources might convey can be essential as the IME provider works to build a set of opinions related to an insured's condition and their functional complaints.

5

Considerations in Structuring the Independent Neuropsychological Evaluation

This chapter focuses on insights related to structuring the neuropsychological IME. A neuropsychological IME differs from a more typical clinical neuropsychological evaluation in important ways. This chapter addresses a range of considerations that may be useful for IME providers as they make alterations to their typical clinical approach to an evaluation.

The chapter assumes that the reader has a fundamental knowledge of neuropsychological assessment in terms of (a) the general scope associated with clinical evaluations, (b) manifestation of neuropsychological difficulties in specific clinical populations, and (c) how to select tests to explore areas of specific neuropsychological strengths and weaknesses and/or emotional functioning. This chapter offers suggestions that may be helpful to the provider of a neuropsychological IME in conceptualizing and structuring the evaluation in order to address unique referral questions that often accompany a request for a neuropsychological IME.

As noted in Chapter 1 of this book, neuropsychological IMEs occur against a medico-legal backdrop; that is, IMEs are performed within the context of an adjudication process and/or dispute resolution, which is often related to some aspect of employment or work-related functionality. The examination processes are typically viewed by both the retaining party and the party undergoing the neuropsychological IME as having very real financial consequences. Indeed, disability benefits are often conceptualized as a financial safety net by those who have purchased policies or have enrolled in disability plans offered by employers or other entities. In addition to evaluations in the context of disability benefits, IMEs are also often requested within the contexts of formal legal disputes. There are a number of excellent texts dedicated to forensic neuropsychological evaluations more generally (e.g., Faust, 2012; Larabee, 2012), and the interested reader is referred to these sources for further discussion of the principles and nuances associated with forensic neuropsychological evaluations.

The neuropsychological IME represents an important tool used to gain a better understanding of how an insured's condition either meets or does not meet a policy/contractual definition of *disability*. In most circumstances, policy definitions revolve around the presence of work-related impairments, limitations, and restrictions driven by a demonstrated association with an illness or injury.

Claims for disability benefits related to behavioral health or neuropsychological conditions are often challenging for those attempting to adjudicate such claims (Waldron, 2003). The challenges are based in large part on the fact that (1) there is no medical litmus test, such as an MRI or lab study, to identify a neuropsychological or behavioral health condition; (2) multiple factors (e.g., preexisting personality traits, level of psychological resiliency, motivation, work setting issues, how one copes with an injury or illness) may contribute to ongoing functional impairment; and (3) there is no clear empirically based classification system for the degree of occupational impairment that one might expect from a neuropsychological or behavioral health condition (Hadjistavropoulos & Bieling, 2001; Lovejoy & Oakes, 2012; Piechowski, 2006). The neuropsychological IME is used to obtain better clarity in understanding the often complex and multifactorial presentations of individuals reporting neuropsychologically based impairments, limitations, and restrictions that relate to work.

Factors That May Impact the Evaluation Structure

Each practitioner commonly structures his or her neuropsychological IMEs in a particular fashion. However, there are multiple aspects of a neuropsychological evaluation that may require some rethinking or change for an IME. Such changes revolve around the central concept that an evaluator is often attempting to comment not only on whether there is a neuropsychological condition that is associated with an impairment, but also whether any identified impairment rises to a level that would create functional limitations in the insured's ability to perform the duties of a particular occupation or, sometimes, even a particular job. The difference between an occupation and a job is discussed in greater detail later in this chapter.

The examiner may need to think flexibly about changing his or her typical approach to an evaluation. These changes typically fall within the following four general areas: (1) changes to the interview for collection of information associated with work-related functionality; (2) changes to the test battery to emphasize areas of work-related concern involving cognition; (3) changes to the test battery to address potential interactions among emotional/psychological and cognitive variables as they relate to the formation and maintenance of potential work-related impairments; and (4) changes to the evaluation frame/process to better evaluate psychometric and non-psychometric issues associated with claimed impairments in functional capacity.

The issues associated with structuring of the neuropsychological IME are reviewed separately in the following sections of this chapter. Many of the changes and considerations are not necessarily required as part of a neuropsychological IME. Rather, the evaluator may find a change or a combination of changes useful in case-by-case situations to generate richer information related to work functionality. There may also be times when referral sources request particular changes for a neuropsychological IME. Before exploring specific changes that are sometimes utilized or requested as part of a neuropsychological IME, it is important to review and understand some of the more typical referral questions associated with these evaluations, as these questions often set the framework for a neuropsychological IME, in terms of focus, scope, and content.

Typical Referral Questions That Inform the Evaluation Structure

The referral questions are typically generated by the insurance carrier/referral source. The questions are typically designed to help the claims adjudicator gather focused information from an IME that will improve the ability to apply contractual policy definitions to the insured's disability claim.

Referral questions are typically phrased as general inquiries. The following question is an example of such a general inquiry:

> Did the evaluation reveal evidence of valid and reliable impairment that would preclude the insured from completing the main duties of his/her occupation?

This type of question has an overarching nature and asks that the neuropsychologist form a clear opinion about whether there is believable evidence to support the existence of neuropsychological impairment. It also requires an opinion related to whether the impairment, if present, rises to a level that would reasonably prevent the insured from performing his or her primary occupational tasks. This question and others like it are often at the heart of most neuropsychological IMEs.

The question requires that the neuropsychologist is familiar with the duties associated with the insured's occupation. This information commonly has been independently verified and forwarded to the neuropsychologist within the IME-related materials for review. If the referral source did not forward a description of the insured's occupational duties, the neuropsychologist will need to gather the information during an interview.

It is important to note here that a distinction is sometimes made between the duties associated with one's occupation and the duties or environment associated with one's job. Particular disability policies may make reference to the duties associated with an occupation. For instance, a particularly stressful work environment characterized by adversarial relationships with a direct manager may have contributed to strong feelings of anxiety for an architect (the occupation) that negatively impacts his or her ability to focus on and complete architectural plans when that manager is present (the specific job). The distinction between a job and an occupation becomes relevant in situations such as this when an impairment and a work-related limitation are uniquely tied to an individual's job. That is, it may be that if the architect were able to obtain a different job within the same occupation, the triggers for the architect's anxious thoughts and poor concentration would no longer be present, allowing him or her to function normally. Conversely, it might also be the case that the manager's behaviors were so severe and the architect's resilience was so low that the anxiety caused by the continuous exposure to these job-related stressors generalized, potentially causing the architect to experience severe anxiety and concentration difficulties across job sites/architectural offices. In this case, there may be evidence for functional impairments and work-related limitations across both the specific job and the broader occupation.

In terms of occupational duties, it is also important to understand not only how the insured functions in the workplace, but also how she relates her perceived impairments to functional difficulties at work. This nexus or interplay between a potential impairment and an individual's ability to perform a task or duty is central to the conceptualization and structure of a neuropsychological IME. Eliciting examples during the interview of such relationships is important in developing a conceptualization of the insured's claimed functional impairments and developing relevant hypotheses to test during the course of a neuropsychological evaluation. For instance, if an office worker with stable multiple sclerosis was asked to describe how his perceived cognitive problems might prevent or interfere with his work, he might respond that he has difficulty processing information fast enough to keep up with daily work, or perhaps may indicate that he becomes overwhelmed by fatigue during the course of the day. This should prompt questions during the interview related to when and under what conditions potential processing speed deficits occur. It should also prompt questions as to whether there are or could be work-related accommodations that could help alleviate such difficulties. Finally, such information should prompt for the inclusion of tests that emphasize abilities that relate to information-processing speed. Of course, an examinee's perceived problems with his cognitive ability, such as processing speed, may actually reflect limitations with other cognitive abilities; therefore testing should not focus solely on the cognitive ability identified by the examinee.

Once the evaluator has an understanding of the insured's work duties and how his or her perceived condition or impairments impact work duties, the evaluator can begin to design a comprehensive test battery that addresses the perceived areas of weakness, as well as any areas of cognitive or emotional strength that might help the insured to compensate for any weaknesses. In arriving at a final opinion related to this form of referral question, the evaluator needs to integrate and reflect upon all of the information collected, including the forwarded IME materials, the interview (and/or collateral interviews), behavioral observations, and the neuropsychological test results. Such information is integrated with the empirical evidence on brain–behavior relationships, rehabilitative and other treatment methods, and functional outcomes.

Other referral questions commonly follow from, or relate to, the primary general referral question. A sample of such questions is provided in Box 5.1.

These questions typically have relevance with regard to policy interpretation and adjudication of the disability claim. Because the concept of "disability" or the state of being "disabled" is viewed by referral sources as a legal and/or contractual concept, it is exceedingly rare for a referral source to ask an evaluator to comment directly upon "disability." Instead, such

Box 5.1 Sample Disability IME Referral Questions

Primary

- Did the evaluation reveal evidence of valid and reliable impairment that would preclude the insured from completing the main duties of his or her occupation?

Secondary

- If impairments and limitations are identified, are the impairments of sufficient duration or intensity to cause a complete cessation of work?
- Does the insured have the capacity to work part-time, in association with the defined occupation?
- Are there reasonable accommodations that would mitigate impairments in the workplace?
- If this individual is unable to function within his or her previous occupation, would the impairments and limitations limit him or her from functioning within a different occupation?
- Does an active psychological or emotional condition cause or contribute to the claimed work-related impairments and limitations?
- Is current treatment related to the impairments appropriate?
- Would adjustments in treatment result in a change in prognosis for functional difficulties?

determinations are ultimately decided by an adjudicator or, in certain situations, the trier of fact. This practice differs from that of many clinical settings in which neuropsychologists opine and sometimes write letters regarding their patients' disability status.

The Neuropsychological Interview

The typical neuropsychological IME includes a thorough evaluation of clinical, motivational, and contextual (e.g., job setting) factors that contribute to an overall understanding of potential work-related functional impairments.

In most instances, this process begins with a review of available records associated with the disability claim file. There is a range of materials that may be sent for review as part of an IME. These materials provide the evaluator with some of the basic information needed to begin to conceptualize and structure the evaluation. For instance, the materials typically describe the symptoms or the condition that has led to the claimed work-related impairments and limitations. The materials may also lend insight into how the insured's treaters conceptualize work-related impairments.

Such information may inform the evaluator about particular information that may need to be obtained during the interview, or topics that require further exploration or understanding. Structuring the interview to include questions and content related to the interaction between the (1) presenting condition and symptoms, (2) reported impairments, (3) reported limitations, (4) proposed restrictions, and (5) workplace environment can be important as one strives to formulate specific opinions about work-related functionality. Typical IME-related topics to be explored within the interview are provided in Box 5.2.

Cognitive Assessment

Reliance on subjective symptom reports in an interview does not, in and of itself, prevent one from rendering a neuropsychological or behavioral health diagnosis that is both valid and reliable (Lovejoy & Oakes, 2012). Such procedures are regularly employed in non-forensic settings that lack the clear potential for secondary gain (American Psychiatric Association, 2013). However, within the medico-legal context of a neuropsychological IME, the sole reliance on this form of information can certainly make matters far more difficult for the claims examiner, especially given the high base rates for symptom exaggeration/distortion in this population.

Research has also found that the difficulties associated with reliance upon self-report extend well beyond accuracy of symptom reporting and the ability to establish a meaningful diagnosis. There is a body of research that demonstrates that people have a tendency to inaccurately report a number of pertinent historical factors. For instance, studies have found that people generally have difficulty with the accurate recall of past medical events/history and associated sick leave (Rogler, Malgady, & Tryon, 1992). Studies have also found difficulties with the accurate recollection/reporting of psychological and neuropsychological histories (Henry,

Box 5.2 Topics Typically Explored in Disability IME Interviews

- How a neuropsychological, medical, or behavioral health diagnosis was initially established
- The symptom course
- How and when the symptoms created functional impairments
- How the neuropsychological condition/symptoms were or are expressed in the workplace
- How the impairments impacted the insured's ability to perform the primary duties associated with his or her occupation
- Whether alterations in the work environment were ever attempted and whether they were helpful in reducing the claimed functional impairments
- Whether, how, and when the impairments manifest outside of the workplace
- Whether the claimed work-related impairments (e.g., nature, severity, and duration) comport with what is known about the typical sequelae/impairments associated with a particular condition or injury
- Whether there are premorbid or comorbid conditions or circumstances that might contribute to the insured's ongoing experience of work-related impairments
- The insured's level of satisfaction or dissatisfaction with his or her occupation and work environment
- The insured's beliefs about length of work impairment
- The insured's beliefs about the possibility of returning to work in the future.

Moffit, Caspi, Langly, & Silva, 1994; Hilsabeck, Gouvier, & Bolter, 1998; Simon & VonKorff, 1995; Widom & Morris, 1997), as well as with past academic performance (Greiffenstein, Baker, & Johnson-Greene, 2002). In most cases, recall biases reflect an underestimation of past/premorbid problems or difficulties, and an overestimation of achievements. However, symptom or historical distortion in the opposite direction is also a potential feature of psychopathology. For example, social psychology studies have revealed that current mood state can contribute to a negative recall bias related to a number of historical facts (e.g., Direnfeld & Roberts, 2006).

The neuropsychological IME is an important tool given the potential vulnerabilities inherent in information-collection methods (particularly in medico-legal arenas) that rely solely on an individual's self-report during an interview; that is, the neuropsychological IME emphasizes objective testing that extends beyond the relatively subjective clinical interview and offers quantifiable methods for evaluating symptom magnification, cognition, behavior, and emotional functioning.

For many years, there has been active debate in the field of neuropsychology as to the strengths and weaknesses of either a fixed battery approach or a flexible battery approach to neuropsychological assessment, particularly within the forensic domain. This debate has been addressed in court as well as in the neuropsychological literature. At present, the opinion of the court, the population of actively practicing neuropsychologists surveyed, and the research literature indicate that a flexible battery approach can be comparable if not superior to the fixed battery approach in terms of its ability to meet the standards for legal evidence, the level of usage among practicing neuropsychologists, and its potential for diagnostic accuracy (Rohling, 2015). As such, the neuropsychologist serving as an IME provider is able to reasonably exercise a choice in terms of assembling a neuropsychological battery to evaluate the neuropsychological complaints of an insured.

Given that IMEs occur within a medico-legal context, the inclusion of both symptom validity and performance validity measures is also important. Lovejoy and Oakes (2012) note that it is essential to examine the credibility of IME assessment data before other IME-related questions can be answered with reasonable insight. Chapter 6 of the present book provides a more thorough discussion of the assessment of validity during a neuropsychological IME.

The nature of the insured's work-related complaints may also guide test selection for a neuropsychological IME.

Psychological Assessment

Referral sources often request that neuropsychologists address the possibility of psychological/psychiatric impairment, in addition to neurocognitive impairment. The ability to evaluate emotional functioning in addition to cognitive functioning, during the same evaluation, creates a distinct advantage for neuropsychological IMEs in helping to comprehensively elucidate the presence or absence of work-related impairments stemming from neuropsychological difficulties. It is common for referral sources to request that an IME provider incorporate measures of personality and emotional functioning that employ validity scales, given the justified concerns about symptom magnification. Referral sources often name specific tests (e.g., MMPI-2-RF) that they want administered, sometimes even requesting a specific computerized interpretation of the results. If neuropsychologists have questions or concerns about the tests or other methods that have been requested, they should contact the referral source to discuss the concerns before commencing with the evaluation.

The presence of a behavioral health condition and/or impairment can be informative regarding how cognitive impairments manifest or become subject to exacerbation in particular circumstances. The inclusion of personality and emotional testing may also aid with the identification of symptoms or conditions that were previously underappreciated within the overall clinical presentation.

There are also circumstances during which a referral source may specifically request an opinion as to whether a behavioral health condition is either causing or contributing to a cognitive or perhaps physical impairment. Such insights may be important with regard to particular policy provisions that exclude impairments related to behavioral health conditions or the exacerbation of other impairments because of the presence of a behavioral health condition. Examples of these interactions include pain that is worsened and/or maintained by the experience of depression, a post-concussive syndrome that is driven by somatization, the experience of palpitations that are caused by anxiety, and so on.

Self-report inventories that help in evaluating an individual's psychological experience of pain may also be useful and/or requested as part of certain neuropsychological IMEs. Some of these measures also have associated scales that address the validity of an individual's self-report of pain quality and intensity.

Changes to the Evaluation Frame/Process

The impairments and work-related limitations that are claimed by an insured may demand different types of IMEs to evaluate for different types of functional impairments. For instance, symptoms of pain and fatigue reported by a plumber may result in difficulties with lifting equipment and/or assuming positions that require a wide range of motion. To address these difficulties, a medical IME may include a physical functional capacity evaluation (FCE) to assess strength, flexibility, and physical endurance. On the other hand, complaints of pain and fatigue reported by an attorney, who has been determined to have a sedentary work capacity, may require a neuropsychological IME to better understand the nature and severity of work-related restrictions and limitations. Individuals who spend much of their day engaged in a high degree of cognitive activity/output often experience cognitive disruption as the primary work-related impairment associated with the experience of pain and/or fatigue. Given that their work involves cognitive output, as opposed to physical output, a neuropsychological evaluation can be the most appropriate method to evaluate how such intrusive symptoms potentially impact the individual's ability to complete his or her cognitively based occupational duties.

In certain cases, the neuropsychological evaluation is also an important tool because it can simulate and measure many of the cognitively based functional activities that individuals with sedentary occupations engage in over the course of workday (e.g., paying attention, learning and retaining new information, cognitively processing new information, problem-solving). If structured correctly, a neuropsychological evaluation requires an individual to engage in active cognitive output over the better part of a day. When viewed in this way, the neuropsychological evaluation becomes a cognitive FCE, during which cognitive complaints, emotional complaints, complaints of fatigue, and complaints of pain can be observed and quantitatively examined during an evaluation that is largely sedentary in nature, during a time frame that approximates a normal workday.

Some neuropsychologists prefer to perform evaluations over shorter blocks of time, with testing procedures intentionally spaced out over the course of days, to minimize the potential confounding effects of factors such as pain and fatigue on cognition and/or emotional functioning. An evaluation structure/frame such as this may actually make it more difficult to measure work-related neuropsychological complaints that are experienced over the course of a workday. In cases like these, a referral source may request that the neuropsychological IME be conducted over the course of a single full day, or over the course of perhaps a day and a half. Having an insured return for neuropsychological testing, following a full day of evaluation the previous day, allows for an extended evaluation of the effects of fatigue on cognitive ability. Such procedures help to better understand complaints of having "good days and bad days," with bad days particularly occurring after days that are reportedly stressful or cognitively taxing. However, neuropsychologists must use care in their interpretation of such evaluations to note at which points in the evaluation low scores were produced. An examinee who performs well on challenging cognitive measures late in the evaluation process is not exhibiting significant fatigue effects, whereas one who performs well on earlier measures but poorly on later measures may well be exhibiting the effects of fatigue if the same cognitive domains were sampled across time points. Adapting the frame of the neuropsychological evaluation in this way allows for day-long observations of potential pain-related behaviors, visible fatigue, or within-day cognitive declines.

Conclusions

The independent neuropsychological evaluation can be a complex undertaking. The neuropsychological IME differs from a clinical neuropsychological evaluation in a number of important ways. There are also a number of potential considerations associated with structuring and conducting such an evaluation that can add to the usefulness of the evaluation results. Each IME is different in terms of the referral questions, the clinical condition in question, the nature of any potential work-related limitations and restrictions, and the interface with conditions such as pain and fatigue. The insights and suggestions in this chapter were designed to help the IME provider navigate these often complex waters, with a greater understanding of the issues and challenges associated with such evaluations.

6

Assessment of Response, Symptom, and Performance Validity

Persons undergoing neuropsychological IMEs often benefit monetarily and/or psychologically when the results reveal impaired abilities and functioning in daily life. As a result, there can be considerable incentive for such persons to present in a manner that supports their claims of impairment and disability. Persons with valid problems may exaggerate their problems or may fabricate additional problems, and persons with no such problems may completely fabricate problems. Research has revealed that invalid responding and performing in forensic contexts in which IMEs are performed are extremely common, with base rates approaching or exceeding 50% (Bush & Graver, 2013; Chafetz, 2008; Larrabee, 2007a). Additionally, effort has been found to have a greater effect than severe brain injury on neuropsychological test performance for claimants seeking compensation (Green, Rohling, Lees-Haley, & Allen III, 2001; Meyers, Volbrecht, Axelrod, & Reinsch-Boothby, 2011).

In addition to over-reporting, exaggerating, or fabricating problems, examinees may benefit from presenting their premorbid status and functioning as being better than it was, or from minimizing or denying problems that they deem unrelated to the primary presenting issue. Doing so helps to enhance post-injury or post-illness problems. Both exaggerating and minimizing problems can mislead examiners and increase the challenges normally encountered when making differential diagnoses with valid information and data.

The ability of neuropsychologists to make statements regarding cognitive and emotional constructs, diagnosis, causality, prognosis, and ability to perform essential work-related activities rests on an informed opinion that the examinee approached the examination in a valid manner, responding honestly to background questions, putting forth good effort on ability measures, and responding truthfully on measures of psychological functioning. However, such "opinion" cannot be based on clinical judgment alone (Guilmette, 2013); a multi-method approach to validity assessment that includes objective, evidence-based psychometric measures must be used and appropriately interpreted. The use of standardized symptom and performance validity measures, combined with objective evidence of response validity, provides the independent examiner the needed evidence for making determinations about the validity of the examinee's approach to the examination and the data obtained.

Response validity refers to the accuracy of the examinee's responses to background questions involving personal history and established or alleged injury or illness (Bush, 2014). Inaccurate historical information can compromise the accuracy of the neuropsychologist's conclusions. *Performance validity* refers to the examinee's engagement or effort to perform well on ability measures such as cognitive and motor tests (Larrabee, 2012). Degree of effort to perform well on such measures influences the validity of the results. Suboptimal performance artificially lowers scores across cognitive ability measures (Armistead-Jehle & Buican, 2012; Fox, 2011; Green, 2007; Green et al., 2001; Lange, Iverson, Brooks, & Rennison, 2010; Meyers et al., 2011) and thus reduces or eliminates the confidence that can be placed in the results of ability measures as being accurate reflections of the constructs of interest. *Symptom validity* refers to the accuracy of the existence, nature, and severity of neuropsychological or medical problems. Fabrication or exaggeration of symptoms interferes with accurate diagnosis and related conclusions and recommendations. Both under- and over-reporting of symptoms interferes with accurate determinations about the examinee.

A comprehensive review of this topic is beyond the scope of this chapter and book. Indeed, entire volumes that summarize the vast scientific and scholarly literature on this topic and advance the practice of validity assessment have been published (e.g., Carone & Bush, 2013; Larrabee, 2007b;

Morgan & Sweet, 2009). In this chapter, we provide a concise overview of relevant concepts and practices. Neuropsychologists performing IMEs will need to review and understand the broader body of literature on validity assessment.

Standard of Care

A multi-method approach to the assessment of validity is the standard of care (Bush et al., 2005b; Heilbronner, Sweet, Morgan, Larrabee, Millis, and Conference Participants, 2009). Although validity assessment measures have been increasingly included in neuropsychological evaluations for many years (Martin, Schroeder, & Odland, 2015), the publication of the position statement by the National Academy of Neuropsychology (Bush et al., 2005) more than a decade ago was a significant step toward establishing the psychometric assessment of effort and honesty as a standard of care for all medically necessary neuropsychological evaluations, with particular importance in evaluation contexts, such as independent examinations, in which the base rate of dissimulation increases. The subsequent position statements by the American Academy of Clinical Neuropsychology (Heilbronner et al., 2009), the British Psychological Society (2009), and the Association for Psychological Advancement in Psychological Injury and Law (Bush, Heilbronner, & Ruff, 2014) provided consensus about the necessity of formal validity assessment. Other relevant position statements have also included statements on the importance of the appropriate assessment of validity (American Educational Research Association, American Psychological Association, & National Council on Measurement in Education, 2014). Thus, at this point, there can be no doubt about the necessity of formal, multi-method assessment of validity in neuropsychological evaluations in general and forensic evaluations, including independent evaluations, in particular.

Ethical Implications

Appropriate assessment of response, symptom, and performance validity is consistent with ethical practice (Bush, 2009, 2013). By extension, failure to use psychometric validity assessment measures in independent neuropsychological examinations is inconsistent with ethical practice. Omission of such measures fails to satisfy APA (2010) Ethical Standards 2.04 (Bases for Scientific and Professional Judgments) and 9.01 (Bases for Assessments). A variety of measures exists to inform neuropsychologists about the validity of an examinee's approach to an IME, but these measures are not equal in terms of psychometric properties and thus usefulness for determining symptom and performance validity. Failure to include in the IME validity assessment measures that have strong psychometric properties does not meet ethical mandates to base opinions on adequate empirical evidence. Similarly, failure to interpret the results of validity assessment measures in a manner consistent with professional literature, whether by over- or understating conclusions about symptom or performance validity, is inconsistent with ethical practice. Neuropsychologists should be able to describe the scientific foundations of their conclusions regarding symptom and performance validity. Competent and well-intentioned neuropsychologists should be able to explain their reasoning and justify their decisions about the inclusion or exclusion of specific validity assessment measures. Because of the evolving nature of validity assessment, neuropsychologists must strive to remain abreast of the advances in this aspect of practice (ES 2.03, Maintaining Competence).

Assessment of Response Validity

Background questions of particular relevance in independent neuropsychological evaluations vary somewhat depending on the purpose and nature of the IME, but typically involve (a) education level and quality; (b) substance use; (c) legal problems or litigation; (d) mental health problems or treatment; (e) prior injuries, illness, and recovery; (f) relevant family history; (g) work history and problems; and (h) onset and course of current problems. Misinformation about one or more of these issues can compromise the accuracy of the neuropsychologist's conclusions. For example, an examinee who reports having graduated from college but in fact had not taken any college courses is likely, because of inappropriate selection of norms based on the misinformation, to be found to have lower cognitive function than is actually the case. Similarly, an examinee who sustained a head injury and reports having been unconscious for 2 hours when in fact he had not lost consciousness at all would be diagnosed with a more severe traumatic brain injury than was actually the case. Examination of relevant records allows neuropsychologists to compare self-reported background with objective evidence; discrepancies raise questions about response validity, whereas consistencies increase the confidence that can be placed in the accuracy of the information.

Assessment of Symptom Validity

There are three general approaches to symptom validity assessment: (1) freestanding measures developed specifically to assess symptom validity; (2) scales or indices that are a component of a more comprehensive measure of psychological functioning, pain, and/or somatic symptoms; and (3) score patterns derived from symptom inventories. Sharland and Gfeller (2007) provided survey data on the validity assessment measures that were most commonly used and considered effective by respondents, as of 2006 when their article was accepted for publication. Martin et al. (2015) provided updated survey data regarding overall use of validity assessment measures and frequency of use of specific measures. They reported a considerable overall increase in the standardized assessment of validity in neuropsychological evaluations. The measures we cover in the following sections include measures that we find to be commonly used and beneficial in IME contexts. Because it is beyond the scope of this chapter to cover all the validity assessment measures covered in prior surveys and other resources, interested readers are referred to the two survey references and more comprehensive volumes (e.g., Boone, 2007; Carone & Bush, 2013; Larrabee, 2007b; Morgan & Sweet, 2009).

Freestanding Symptom Validity Measures

Freestanding symptom validity measures often appear to be assessing problems or abilities of concern to examinees, such as problems with memory or psychological distress, but, by comparing score patterns or profiles to various research or clinical samples known to have over-endorsed problems, actually provide information about the validity of the reported symptoms. Limitations of freestanding measures are that they require additional test administration time and, because they can become readily identified as validity measures, may be more susceptible to coaching than are indices embedded within tests of other constructs.

One example within the cognitive realm, the Memory Complaints Inventory (MCI; Green, 2003) is a computer-administered 58-item measure of subjective memory complaints. Responses are represented in the following nine scales: General Memory Problems (GMP), Numeric Information Problems (NIP), Visuospatial Memory Problems (VSMP), Verbal Memory Problems (VMP), Pain Interferes with Memory (PIM), Memory Interferes with Work (MIW), Impairment of Remote Memory (IRM), Amnesia for Complex

Behavior (ACB), and Amnesia for Antisocial Behavior (AAB). The first six scales assess complaints of memory difficulties that can have a neurologic basis, whereas the final three scales identify memory complaints that are non-neurologic in origin. The scores for the various scales can be compared to a variety of patient and simulator groups that have valid or invalid profiles.

An example within the psychological realm, the Structured Inventory of Malingered Symptomatology (SIMS; Widows & Smith, 2005) is a 75-item true–false measure developed to assess feigned psychiatric and neurologic problems. Responses are grouped into the following five scales, which are considered common targets of feigned symptomatology: Low Intelligence (LI), Affective Disorders (AF), Neurologic Impairment (NI), Psychosis (P), and Amnesia (AM), and a total score is calculated. A meta-analytic investigation provided support for the ability of the SIMS to discriminate between feigning and honest responders (van Impelen, Merckelbach, Jelicic, & Merten, 2014). The original total cutoff score of > 14 has been found to have unacceptable false positive rates, prompting recommendations for use of ≥ 23 as a preferred cutoff (Boone, 2013). Concern has also been raised about low specificity.

Embedded Validity Scales and Indices

Unlike freestanding measures of symptom validity, embedded measures are included within measures of actual psychological symptomatology. For example, the Minnesota Multiphasic Personality Inventory (MMPI) in its various forms is the most widely used measure for assessing personality and psychopathology by neuropsychologists (Rabin, Barr, & Burton, 2005) and the most commonly used measure of symptom validity by neuropsychologists (Martin et al., 2015; Sharland & Gfeller, 2007). Either the MMPI-2 (Butcher, Dahlstrom, Graham, Tellegen, & Kaemmer, 1989) or the MMPI-2-RF (Ben-Porath & Tellegen, 2008) is a staple in the test battery of most neuropsychologists performing IMEs and is commonly required by many IME referral sources.

Most clinicians learn early in their psychology graduate training that the first step in the interpretation of the MMPI is determining whether the results are valid. In addition to the core validity scales that have long been part of the MMPI, new scales have been developed and have been integrated into the measure over the years. Many of the newer scales have focused on somatic, including neurologic/cognitive, symptoms that are particularly relevant in personal injury and disability examination contexts. Because of its relatively recent development and the observation that many practitioners are using the restructured form, only the MMPI-2-RF's approach to validity assessment is covered here.

The MMPI-2-RF, composed of 338 true–false items, provides three approaches to the assessment of validity: content non-responsiveness, under-reporting, and over-reporting (Ben-Porath & Tellegen, 2008). Content non-responsiveness targets the examinee's understanding of test items with the Cannot Say (CNS), Variable Response Inconsistency (VRIN-r), and True Response Inconsistency (TRIN-r) scales. Patterns of responding consist of either excessive variability or invariability. Possible explanations for excessive variability (VRIN-r) include poor understanding of item content (e.g., reduced reading comprehension) or an intentionally uncooperative approach to the test. The most likely explanation for excessive fixed responding (TRIN-r) is an uncooperative approach to the test. Symptom under-reporting is assessed with the Uncommon Virtues (L-r) and Adjustment Validity (K-r) scales. Elevations on L-r and K-r reflect a self-presentation that is highly favorable and well adjusted, typically with an absence of psychopathology. Symptom over-reporting is assessed with the Infrequent Responses (F-r), Infrequent Psychopathology Responses (Fp-r), Infrequent Somatic Responses (Fs), Symptom Validity (FBS-r), Response Bias (RBS), and the Henry-Heilbronner Index (HHI-r) scales. Examination of these validity scales informs the neuropsychologist about both the examinee's approach to the evaluation and the ability to interpret the clinical scales.

The Personality Assessment Inventory (PAI; Morey, 1991), composed of 344 items, provides eight scales designed to determine the validity of the results. Four of the scales were initially included, and four scales were subsequently added. As with the MMPI-2-RF, the PAI validity scales assess content non-responsiveness, denial or under-reporting of problems, and symptom over-reporting. Non-responsiveness is assessed with the Inconsistency (INC) and Infrequency (INF) scales. Denial or under-reporting of symptoms is assessed with the Positive Impression Management (PIM) scale, Defensiveness Index (DEF), and Cashel Discriminant Function (CDF). Symptom over-reporting is assessed with the Negative Impression Management (NIM) scale, Malingering Index (MAL), and Rogers Discriminant Function (RDF).

The Battery for Health Improvement 2 (BHI 2) is a multidimensional biopsychosocial inventory of persons with chronic pain composed of 63 multiple-choice items (Bruns & Disorbio, 2014). "The BHI 2 utilizes two separate validity conditions to determine whether or not a protocol can be meaningfully interpreted. The first condition has to do with bizarre responding, while the second has to do with failure to respond (i.e., leaving items blank)" (p. 343). Two scales are used to assess bizarre responding. The first scale assesses Defensiveness. High defensiveness scores suggest a positive bias ("faking good"), whereas low scores suggest a negative bias ("faking bad"). The second scale, Self-Disclosure, was developed to assess how much a patient is willing to disclose about internal psychological distress. High Self-Disclosure scores indicate that the patient is disclosing an unusually high level of information about psychological dysfunction, sometimes because he or she is seeking help, but very high scores may be an indication of malingering. Low scores suggest an atypical lack of psychological difficulties, consistent with a tendency to be more psychologically guarded and private, possibility due to concerns about who has access to the information that will be disclosed. There are also other indications of malingering embedded within the clinical scales. For example, very high scores on the Symptom Dependency and Perseverance scales have been associated with malingering. Despite these valuable findings, more research is needed on the use of the BHI 2 for determinations of malingering.

Symptom Inventory Score Patterns

The Neurobehavioral Symptom Inventory (NSI) is a 22-item self-report measure of physical, cognitive, emotional, and behavioral symptoms commonly reported following a concussion (Cicerone & Kalmar, 1995). The NSI is widely used and researched with veterans (Benge, Pastorek, & Thornton, 2009; Soble et al., 2014; Vanderploeg et al., 2014). Vanderploeg et al. (2014) developed three validity scales from the NSI items: Negative Impression Management (NIM5) based on five unusual items, Low-Frequency (LOW6) based on six items that are infrequently endorsed by valid responders, and the combination of 10 non-overlapping items (Validity-10). The following cutoff scores, balancing sensitivity and specificity, were identified for these three embedded scales and the total NSI score: NIM5 > 12, LOW6 > 13, Validity-10 > 22, and NSI total score > 58. Additional research on the NSI validity scales is needed.

Assessment of Performance Validity

As with symptom validity assessment, there are three general approaches to the psychometric assessment of an examinee's effort to perform well on cognitive tests: (1) freestanding tests developed specifically to assess performance validity; (2) empirically derived indicators embedded within cognitive ability tests; and (3) actuarial formulas calculated from performance on cognitive ability tests. All three approaches help identify illogically low or inconsistent performances that clearly or potentially invalidate performance on neuropsychological ability tests. Despite intuitive concerns, the empirical evidence does not support the idea that the administration of more performance validity tests (PVTs), in and of itself, increases the likelihood of multiple PVT failures (Berthelson et al., 2013; Davis & Millis, 2014); thus, the evidence does not support placing a cap on the number of PVTs included in a battery. When clear evidence of suboptimal performance is obtained during test administration, the neuropsychologist must decide whether to complete or discontinue the evaluation. In most IME contexts, it is advisable to complete the evaluation so that all expected information can be gathered and integrated into conclusions.

Freestanding Performance Validity Tests

The survey by Sharland and Gfeller (2007) revealed that the Test of Memory Malingering (TOMM; Tombaugh, 1996), Validity Indicator Profile (VIP; Frederick & Crosby, 2000), and Word Memory Test (WMT; Green, Allen, & Astner, 1996) were the three most commonly used freestanding PVTs at that time. Martin et al. (2015) found the TOMM, WMT, and Medical Symptom Validity Test (MSVT; Green, 2005) to be the three PVTs used most frequently by respondents, in that order. Our experience is consistent with the findings of Martin et al. (2015); that is, the TOMM and WMT are the most widely used freestanding PVTs, with many other good instruments, including the VIP, also in common use. The Word Choice test, which is part of Pearson's Advanced Clinical Solutions (ACS; Holdnack & Drozdick, 2009) for the WAIS-IV (Wechsler, 2008a) and WMS-IV (Wechsler, 2008b), is one of the most recently published validity tests and seems to be increasing in popularity. Curiously, some measures known to lack sensitivity, such as the Rey 15-Item Test (Rey, 1941), also remain in use by 16% of the Martin et al. respondents, perhaps because of their strong specificity. It is typically recommended that more than one freestanding PVT be used in comprehensive neuropsychological IMEs and that validity assessment measures be disbursed throughout the test battery.

The TOMM is a visually based forced-choice test consisting of two learning trials and an optional retention trial. Per the test manual, scores on

Trial 2 and Retention of 45 or higher is consistent with adequate effort. However, subsequent studies have demonstrated that healthy control subjects and many patient populations obtain perfect or near-perfect scores on those trials (Iverson et al., 2007). Additional scoring paradigms have also been developed, including use of (a) the score from Trial 1 (Denning, 2012), (b) the number of consecutively correct responses to the first 10 items (Denning, 2012), and (c) consistency of responding to the same items across trials (Gunner, Miele, Lynch, & McCaffrey, 2012). Most important, comparison of a given examinee's scores to those of appropriate patient and research groups is needed, rather than simply using the cutoff score provided in the test's manual.

The WMT, initially available as an orally administered test, was subsequently adapted for computer use (Green, 2003; Green et al., 1996). The WMT is a forced choice test involving words. WMT scores have general pass/fail classifications for immediate recall, delayed recall, and consistency across trials. Scores for additional subtests (Multiple Choice, Paired Associates, Free Recall, Long Delayed Free Recall) are also provided. In addition to the general pass/fail classifications, considerable additional value comes from the direct comparisons that can be made to a variety of patient and non-patient samples via the publisher's computerized scoring program, as well as from the large independent literature that exists on this test.

Despite their considerable value for establishing adequate performance validity and detecting suboptimal performance, there are two primary drawbacks to using freestanding PVTs. First, they add administration time to what often is an already lengthy evaluation process. The added time can be taxing for persons experiencing significant neurocognitive or psychiatric disorders. Second, compared to embedded indicators, freestanding PVTs are more easily identified, making at least some of them more susceptible to coaching (Gervais, Green, Allen III, & Iverson, 2001), which is relatively common in forensic contexts (Gervias et al., 2001; Youngjohn, 1995).

Embedded Performance Validity Measures

Given the explosion of research on this topic in the past decade or so, there are now dozens of variables embedded within commonly used cognitive tests and batteries, as well as based on standardized sensory and motor tests, that inform neuropsychologists about performance validity.

Martin et al. (2015) found that 96% of respondents use some apsect of the WAIS-III/IV Digit Span subtest, including 84% who use Reliable Digit Span. Second most frequently used were variables from the California Verbal Learning Test-second edition (CVLT-II), with 75% of respondents using some aspect of that measure, including 58% who use the Forced Choice task. Practitioners are encouraged to review the various texts on neuropsychological assessment of malingering (e.g., Carone & Bush, 2013; Larrabee, 2007b; Morgan & Sweet, 2009), as well as the relevant emerging scientific literature, for those specific tests that are part of their own batteries. Having a readily available list of one's commonly used tests, the embedded indicators for each of the tests, and the cutoff scores for each indicator for commonly encountered patient populations can facilitate determinations of performance validity.

Statistical Formulas

Statistical models applied to cognitive test scores can help examiners determine performance validity. Discriminant function analysis (DFA), multiple regression analysis, and logistic regression are examples of such approaches. Predictive algorithms have been developed for some cognitive tests, allowing examiners to insert relevant test scores, perform a calculation, and obtain a result that can then be compared to values for prediction of adequate or suboptimal effort. Use of statistical formulas, like the embedded measures, has the advantage of not requiring additional test administration time. However, weaknesses also exist. For example, DFA assumes that variables have normal distributions and that groups have equal variances, which is often not the case with performance validity measures, and logistic regression models are very sensitive to the unique characteristics of the tests' validation samples. For these reasons, Miller et al. (in press) recommended caution in the use of such models in clinical and forensic contexts.

The Process

Validity assessment is woven throughout the evaluation process. All aspects of an IME, from the records reviewed to the interview(s) and observations to performance on psychometric measures, inform determinations about the validity of the examinee's presentation and reported problems. Slick and Sherman (2013) described the importance of considering (in)consistencies across these different sources of information.

Some questions emerge regarding aspects of the validity assessment process. Two questions that experience suggests are commonly encountered in practice are as follows.

How Many Validity Assessment Measures Should be Administered?

The specific measures and number of measures should be guided by the evaluation context and the purpose of the evaluation. Martin et al. (2015) found that survey respondents relied on more validity measures in forensic contexts (e.g., IMEs) than clinical contexts. They found that in forensic contexts, an average of 2.4 (range 0 to 6) stand-alone PVTs were used, and 3.9 (range 0 to 12) embedded indicators were considered, for a total of 6.3 (range 0 to 16). Clearly, the practitioners reporting zero PVT use in forensic contexts were not practicing in a manner that is consistent with current standards of practice. It is reasonable to wonder whether the number of validity measures that are administered affect the likelihood of obtaining positive (invalid) results. Because of their low ceiling, PVTs generate a narrow dispersion of scores in a highly skewed distribution, which substantially limits the possibility of obtaining a positive result by chance alone (Miller et al., in press). Miller et al. state, "As long as the intercorrelations among measures remain adequately low, there is currently no empirical data to support a ceiling on the number of validity measures to administer. . ."

How Many Validity Test Failures are Needed to Determine Overall Invalid Performance?

Neuropsychologists use a variety of methods for determining when an examinee's overall performance is considered invalid. Martin et al. (2015) found that the most commonly used method (endorsed by 35% of respondents) requires failure on two or more validity measures that have minimal shared variance.

Should Testing be Discontinued Upon Clear Evidence of Suboptimal Performance?

In IME contexts, experience indicates that most referral sources prefer that neuropsychological evaluations be completed as planned, even when there is clear evidence that the examinee is performing at a suboptimal level. Meaningful information can sometimes be gleaned by reviewing the examinee's performance, even when suboptimal early in the process, over an extended period of time. Martin et al. (2015) found that 70% of forensic practitioners always or often complete the evaluation despite evidence of suboptimal performance. Nineteen percent of forensic practitioners always or often confront or warn examinees who appear to be performing at a suboptimal level. In clinical contexts, neuropsychologists are much more likely to discontinue evaluations early and are somewhat more likely to confront or warn suboptimal performers.

Interpretation

The selection and administration of validity assessment measures and calculation of validity assessment values are typically the easiest and most straightforward part of the validity assessment process, and the part of the process about which most practitioners agree. Interpretation of the results tends to be a more complex process, requiring a good-faith effort to consider multifaceted data and information in an objective manner. It is the interpretation of the results that typically results in the greatest disagreement among practitioners in adversarial contexts. However, experience suggests that such disagreement, while often couched in clinical or scientific terms, typically results more from advocacy or bias in favor of the retaining party than from an objective rendering of the scientific and professional literature. Familiarity with and adherence to scientifically supported best practices serve neuropsychologists well when performing IMEs. We address some of the issues and challenges involved with interpretation of SVT and PVT results in the form of questions.

Is There Evidence of Invalid Test Results?

The first step in the interpretation process is determining whether the obtained SVT and PVT scores are more consistent with valid or invalid performance. Selecting a priori appropriate comparison groups and cutoff scores for use with the current examinee's scores is necessary. Such scores should match as closely as possible the characteristics and presenting problems of the examinee, as well as other groups known to be more severely limited and groups known to have been simulating suboptimal performance. For example, using a cutoff score of 45 for Trial 2 of TOMM for a community-dwelling adult with fibromyalgia, chronic pain, and emotional distress may be inappropriate given the evidence demonstrating near perfect scores (Trial 2 mean = 49.8, SD = 0.5) for such persons who put forth adequate effort. In such a case, use of a cutoff score of 45 would be insensitive to suboptimal effort by persons scoring in the 45 to 48 range. Similarly, when an examinee with persistent post-concussion syndrome who achieves a PVT score that is significantly worse than groups of patients with a history of severe traumatic brain injury (TBI), the PVT performance should be considered evidence of suboptimal performance.

What Do Invalid PVT Scores Mean for Interpretation of the Cognitive Ability Tests?

Based on empirical studies and survey data, the current most widely accepted practice is that failed performance on two or more PVTs precludes consideration of cognitive ability tests as representative of the constructs they otherwise assess (Larrabee, 2008; Martin et al., 2015; Meyers & Volbrecht, 2003). However, care should be taken when applying this two-PVT-failure guideline. Miller et al. (in press), explain that "the cumulative false-positive rate is dependent upon: 1) the number of validity measures interpreted, 2) the psychometric properties of each validity measure, and 3) the association between each measure." They further note the following:

> Although combinations of specific measures and cut scores for multiple failures published by Larrabee (2008) and Victor, Boone, Serpa, Buehler, and Ziegler (2009) perform well, that should not lead to the conclusion that any combination of validity indices is adequate for identification of suboptimal effort across settings . . . [W]hen using multiple PVTs to assess for overall test battery validity, it is useful to empirically study the test operating characteristics in the local (or similar) setting, to ensure that the relationship between validity measures is low and that classification accuracy is comparable to published empirical studies . . . [W]hen using a decision rule of "two or more failures," one should not be counting across both performance and symptom validity measures, or using multiple indices from the same measure.

Despite the extensive empirical evidence and widely accepted practice guidelines, some practitioners, often according to the side by which they were retained, go to great lengths to either explain away failures on validity assessment measures or to attribute generally adequate SVT or PVT performance to an invalid approach to the evaluation. Such efforts often result from professional incompetence or bias. As IME reports are commonly subject to critical peer review, examiners should be prepared to support their validity assessment opinions and conclusions with the underlying research.

Do Invalid SVT Results Invalidate Cognitive Test Results?

Some practitioners state that scores from cognitive ability tests cannot be accepted as valid because of invalid scores on SVTs such as the MMPI-2-RF validity scales. Likewise, some practitioners argue that poor performance on PVTs necessarily invalidates the psychological test results. However, the results of PVTs and SVTs do not necessarily generalize from one to the other. For example, claimants pursuing benefits or compensation for psychological distress may be motivated to exaggerate psychological problems but have little incentive to appear cognitively compromised. Factor analysis supports a distinction between performance and symptom validity (Van Dyke, Millis, Axelrod, & Hanks, 2013). The position of the National Academy of Neuropsychology is that "[i]nvalid performance on a measure of personality does not allow for an a priori conclusion that the neurocognitive test results are also unreliable, and vice versa" (Bush et al., 2005, p. 424). Miller et al. (in press) state clearly, "To assume that cognitive data are invalid as a result of failed symptom validity measures would extend beyond the appropriate use of the measures." Although the literature on this topic is somewhat varied, the consensus remains that a multifactorial approach that includes both types of validity assessment is needed (Bush et al., 2005; Heilbronner et al., 2009; Van Dyke, Millis, Axelrod, & Hanks, 2013).

What do Discrepancies Among the Various Sources of Data Indicate?

Discrepancies between test data and known patterns of brain functioning, and between self-report and documented history, known patterns of brain functioning, behavioral observations, and information from collateral sources are relatively uncommon with valid presentations and therefore provide evidence of an invalid presentation (Slick, Sherman, & Iverson, 1999). Neuropsychologists performing IMEs consider these various factors and whether there are consistencies among the information obtained. The number and significance of the inconsistencies contribute to the examiner's decision about whether an examinee's overall presentation is invalid.

What do I Make of Invalid Data?

Triers of fact and other legal and administrative decision-makers typically want binary conclusions. They want to know in black-and-white terms whether the examinee was malingering. They typically do not consider it helpful to their purposes to hear something along the lines of, "Well, it's a complex, multifaceted situation... ." Fortunately, because the evidence does not always, or even often, lend itself to a clear-cut, unambiguous conclusion of invalid effort or answers, the Slick et al. (1999) criteria provide a structured approach to decision-making that includes specific criteria and probabilistic language. Use of such language when making determinations about malingered neurocognitive dysfunction helps neuropsychologists educate the decision-maker or referral source about issues of concern while remaining sensitive to error rates and the always present risk of false-positive findings. There are many reasons for invalid responding or performance on neuropsychological tests, of which malingering is one (Iverson, 2008). A convergence of evidence in favor of one conclusion or another helps establish the confidence that can be placed in the conclusion.

Occasionally, an examinee's validity assessment results are so extreme that the conclusion about symptom or performance validity is clear. For example, producing scores on forced choice tests that are statistically below chance (e.g., ≤ 17 correct on a test with 50 trials or ≤ 6 on a test with 20 trials) is strong evidence of intent to perform poorly. Nevertheless, the examiner must consider whether other factors, such as misunderstanding the instructions, led to the poor performance. Even if the intent was to perform poorly, it may be difficult to establish the reason underlying the intent. In secondary gain contexts, the monetary reward or benefit would typically be expected to be the driving cause; however, a desire to be uncooperative because of anger at the IME context, or an unconscious or severe psychiatric etiology, may also be possible. Adherence to objective evidence, base rates, and diagnostic criteria serves neuropsychologists, their referral sources, and the ultimate decision-makers well.

Conclusions

Establishing the validity of the examinee's presentation and test performance is a qualitative and quantitative process that occurs throughout the course of the neuropsychological examination. Determining symptom and performance validity is the first step in the interpretation of the test results and informs conclusions about the examinee's neuropsychological functioning. Failure to adequately assess response, symptom, and performance validity reflects suboptimal professional behavior as an independent neuropsychologist. Neuropsychologists who strive to understand an examinee's neuropsychological abilities and deficits through the lens of appropriate validity assessment can make valuable contributions to the forensic decision-making process.

7

Interpretation

The integration of medical records, collateral sources of information, clinical interview, and test findings, in the context of an IME, often presents the greatest challenge in rendering useful, accurate, and reliable opinions regarding an individual's functional capacity. Although a full discussion of specific tests and their interpretation is beyond the scope of this chapter, it is important for IME providers to be aware of potential challenges to interpretation of the various forms of data collected during the evaluation that can arise from flaws in the decision-making process (see Piechowski, 2015). This chapter addresses some of the more common challenges that may arise during the course of interpreting and integrating different forms of data into thoughtful IME-related opinions associated with an individual's functionality. In this chapter, the authors will introduce various concerns in the form of questions. These are the concerns that the authors encounter most often from neuropsychologists providing IMEs. The concerns raised often relate to the integration of complex data during and after an IME has been completed. The issues typically involve several primary areas that may be conceptualized as follows:

1. Concerns about how to psychometrically structure a neuropsychological IME;
2. Concerns about issues that arise during the course of an IME that may impact interpretation of the IME data;

3. Concerns about how to interpret psychometric data in the context of an IME;
4. Concerns about how to interpret and integrate collateral forms of data obtained during the IME process.

The authors acknowledge that there are often multiple ways to approach many of these concerns. As such, the broader goals of this chapter are to make neuropsychological providers aware of some of the more common concerns that impact IME interpretation and to encourage a thoughtful approach to interpreting and integrating various forms of data into one's final IME-related opinions.

Pre-evaluation Psychometric Considerations

Are There Common Psychometric Concerns Associated with the Interpretation of Evaluation Data that I Should be Aware of as I Think About Constructing a Neuropsychological Battery?

From a psychometric standpoint, there are two broad issues that should be considered before beginning the evaluation. The first issue involves the selection of appropriate and demographically relevant, normative data. At times, an IME provider may be tempted to employ a more obscure test and/or normative sample that seems potentially relevant to a referral question. Selection of idiosyncratic test measures or test administration protocols provides data that may be more difficult to interpret in a reliable and valid fashion, within the context of an IME. Use of more obscure tests and normative samples may result in concerns being raised by consultants associated with the referral source or with IME vendors who might perform a quality review of an IME report, prior to its final submission to the referral source.

Second, the issue of whether a profile of neuropsychological test scores reflects the presence of impairment or whether it reflects the presence of normal variability can be a fairly common interpretive struggle during a neuropsychological IME. Providers should certainly be aware that "normal individuals" can demonstrate actual impairments across multiple tests during a neuropsychological evaluation (Binder, Iverson, & Brooks, 2009).

The actual number of low scores obtained by an examinee can depend upon a number of important variables, including (a) how one actually defines a low score, (b) demographic variables (e.g., age, sex, education, and ethnicity), (c) the person's overall level of intellectual functioning, (d) the actual number of tests administered, and (e) the level of intercorrelation between and among tests. Each of these variables should be considered as one develops an interpretive strategy to address an examinee's test scatter.

Oakes, Lovejoy, Holdnack, and Tartar (2013) offer suggestions related to the interpretation of test scatter. Most important is consideration of the clinical context in which the individual presents, including educational and occupational history. The integration of clinical experience and expertise with empirical research related to a test or tests is the essence of evidence-based medicine and neuropsychological assessment/treatment.

Integration of Complex Information

Can I Just Use My Typical Clinical Neuropsychological Battery in an IME?

The simple and most likely answer to this question is "no." The neuropsychological testing for an IME may, and likely should, differ from that of typical test battery given in a clinical context. First, as mentioned elsewhere is this text, the base rates for suboptimal performance in medico-legal contexts are significantly higher than those seen in clinical referrals. As such, much more thorough and continuous assessment of symptom and performance validity is indicated over the course of an IME. Second, much of the emphasis in a clinical examination may involve the questions and processes associated with differential diagnosis. In an IME, the underlying diagnosis may be apparent, and the process of determining the presence or absence of functional impairment is often paramount. Further, IME providers may find that that existing normative data for their commonly used tests may be inadequate in any particular IME depending on demographic factors. Additionally, an understanding of the normal variability that occurs within a test and within a test battery is of critical importance. IME examiners would be well served to make every effort prior to employing a test (and/or test battery) to become familiar with the psychometric properties of the tests to be employed.

For example, there is a strong body of research that describes normal variability using the Extended Halstead-Reitan Battery (Bornstein, 1986; Elias et al., 1990; Heaton, 2004; Heaton et al., 1991; Steinmeyer, 1986), the Meyers Neuropsychological Battery, and the Neuropsychological Assessment Battery (NAB) that may make the use of these batteries more palatable or preferable to an examiner than the use of an idiosyncratic flexible battery for which such data may not be available. While there has historically been concern regarding higher false-positive rates when employing a flexible battery approach (i.e., Orsini et al., 1988), there is a growing body of research to help in understanding false-positive rates in the context of flexible batteries (e.g., Iverson et al., 2012; Palmer et al., 1998). It should also be noted that there is blossoming research regarding normal variability within specific testing instruments that an IME examiner may want to remain abreast of. A good example of this literature is the more recent research regarding the normative data from the WAIS-IV and WMS-IV (Holdnack et al., 2013) that provides a variety of methods and data for comparing obtained variability of a single examinee with that seen in the normative sample and/or specific clinical groups.

In summary, the reliance on one's typical clinical test battery, based on convenience, may not be the soundest approach in association with performing an IME. A careful consideration of the existing literature when determining a test battery is both scientifically and ethically prudent.

Given the Range of Individuals Who Might Review My Report, How Do I Interpret and Describe the Test Findings in a Manner that can be Understood by a Potentially Varied Audience, with Respect to their Understanding of Test Data?

There remains a wide range of styles, formats, and terminology for understanding test performance and describing test scores in neuropsychological reports. In our view, the terminology provided in Table 7.1 provides a useful format for reporting scores.

Table 7.1 Descriptive Terminology by Level of Performance

DESCRIPTOR	INDEX SCORE RANGE	PERCENTILE RANGE
Extremely high	133 and above	99th and above
Very high	124–132	95th–98th
High average	115–123	84th–94th
Average	86–114	18th–82nd
Low average	85–77	16th–6th
Very low	76–68	5th–2nd
Extremely low	67 and below	1st and below

From Stucky & Bush (2017). Used with permission of Oxford University Press.

In addition to providing consistent descriptors for test scores, it is important to have a clear demarcation in one's report between the reporting of scores and the interpretation of scores. All too often, scores are reported in relation to a presumed baseline level of function that may or not actually reflect the full range of an individual's premorbid function. A danger of commenting on single scores is misleading the reader into the perception that a functional deficit is being asserted, rather than noting an abnormal score (which may represent normal variability, an outlier score when compared to others within a functional domain, or an actual functional impairment). As one's verbiage tends to be parsed by various consumers of an IME report, a more economical approach is make a clear delineation between the reporting of scores and the interpretation of such.

To Complete this Evaluation I have Consented to the Presence of a Third Party; How do I Interpret the Data in this Context?

Despite appropriate reservations regarding the presence of a third party, legal precedents are making this an increasingly problematic issue in several jurisdictions. Ideally, prior to consenting to the presence of a third party, an IME evaluator has made the referring party aware of the potential impact of this presence on performance. In addition to citing the published findings regarding the inverse impact on high- and low-difficulty tests (e.g., Gavett, Lynch, & McCaffrey, 2006; Lynch, 2005), the fact that the impact of third-party presence on any particular specific test (or subtest) is not known will need to be acknowledged. It is important to include in one's report a clear description of any third-party attendance, involvement or lack thereof of the observer throughout the assessment process, perceived impact of the third party on the claimant's cooperation and forthrightness, and one's best understanding of the potential impact of the third party on any obtained test findings (Duff & Fisher, 2005). Sample language might include the following:

> Please note that qualifications are added in relation to the results and opinions offered in this report. Third-party influences were present during this evaluation in the form of [*insert specific type of presence*]. All parties were informed that such presence might impact on cognitive test results. They were also informed that determining the exact impact of this presence on performance can be difficult. As such, the opinions associated with this evaluation are offered with caution.

How Does One Interpret Test Findings in the Context of Questionably Valid or Clearly Invalid Performance or Symptom Reporting?

As explained earlier in the book (see Chapter 6), the base rate for invalid performance or symptom validity in the context of IMEs can be quite high, at the 40%–50% range. As such, the issue of interpretation of test findings with potentially unreliable or invalid data is one of the most common issues facing IME providers. One potential model for navigating one's thinking in this regard is to pose a series of questions (see Box 7.1).

The Slick et al. (Slick, Sherman, & Iverson, 1999) model provides a clear conceptual framework by which to classify questionable or clearly invalid performance using probabilistic language. In their more recent work, Slick and Sherman (2013) provide further guidance on the differential diagnosis of malingering and have revised the exclusionary criteria described in the initial model.

Some examiners attempt to integrate "within normal limits" results as demonstrating "at least able" with respect to performance. That is, intact

Box 7.1 Model for Score Interpretation

1. Did the performance on forced choice validity tests yield results at significantly less than chance, consistent with the intentional exaggeration or feigning of deficits?
2. Were scores on the freestanding and embedded performance validity measures clearly consistent with invalid performance?
3. Is there any indication that performance validity scores were below cutoffs due to a genuine impairment (psychological or cognitive) or situational or environmental factors?
4. Did the claimant perform in the normal range on cognitive abilities measures that are similar to performance validity measures for which below cutoff scores were obtained? For example, did the claimant score in the average range on memory tests but below cutoffs on the TOMM?
5. Is there collateral information that is consistent with the exaggeration or feigning of deficits?

performances are noted as demonstrating some level of retained functional capacity, but poor performances are noted as not reliable estimates of actual functional impairment. Such an approach can help maximize the utility of the data obtained (assuming some areas of intact performance). However, descriptions of scores on ability tests that seem to be consistent with invalid performance are often misinterpreted by lay audiences who do not understand the explanation provided in the report. Given the varied audience for an IME report, the evaluator is cautioned to remain aware of the possibility that invalid scores may be interpreted as reflecting actual ability levels and should make their best attempt to provide a clear and comprehensive report that reduces this possibility (for example, a very clear statement such as "In light of clear indications of invalid performance during this examination, the presence of scores below levels of expectancy cannot be construed as valid indicators of the claimant's actual ability level").

How do I Integrate Results of Surveillance, Social Media Searches, or Other Collateral Data that Raise Concern Regarding Symptom Validity?

For the purposes of an IME, collateral information can be of value in providing additional context to the medical records, interview, and test results. However, examiners should exert reasonable caution in the weight and faith put into collateral data. With respect to surveillance, video monitoring at best provides a snapshot of behavior at a particular time and place. Such information may be particularly relevant with respect to asserted physical restrictions or limitations, but rarely does such data provide much evidence regarding an individual's cognitive or psychiatric capacity. Exceptions can include evidence of engaging in specifically denied behaviors, such as the ability to be present in certain locations (crowds, in an elevator, or in the presence of specific "triggering phenomenon"), or the ability to remain active for long periods of time when issues such as depression, motivation, and fatigue are asserted as significant impairments. Caution is urged when considering interpreting video data with respect to emotional status. It is also important to be aware of the format of the data that are being provided: Are you reviewing the raw surveillance data, or are you being provided with someone's interpretation of the data?

Social media searches may also be found within the records sent to an IME provider. These searches can often provide behavioral data that are worth exploring further during an interview. For instance, one may not expect to see that an individual with claimed work impairment such as low energy and anhedonia regularly engages in extreme sports.

IME providers need not be investigators. Insurance carriers typically either do or arrange their own investigations, and having IME providers engage in such activities can become problematic for the carrier that arranged the IME. From experience, it is rare for such behavior to be perceived as having been conducted to assist with supporting a claimant's assertion of impairment, but rather to refute such assertions, which is likely to be reasonably perceived as reflecting a bias on the part of the examiner. For these reasons, examiners are discouraged from conducting their own internal or other electronic searches regarding an examinee.

An IME provider should be aware of potential issues in revealing information obtained from collateral sources (such as surveillance or social media searches) that have been provided for their review. One does not have any ethical obligation to reveal to the claimant that such data have been provided, but ideally the clinical interview would include questions that address discrepancies between self-reported and observed behaviors.

On the other hand, the active solicitation of additional information from collateral sources such as a spouse or a coworker does require a valid authorization for this purpose. Based on experience, collateral information from a spouse or other knowledgeable person regarding the claimant's day-to-day functioning can be of some benefit in elucidating asserted deficits. The obtaining of data from other collateral sources (i.e., employer) may best be handled by the insurance company, which employs individuals who serve this role in the disability process.

At times, disability insurance carriers temporarily withhold and later provide collateral information for consideration. The rationale for such a strategy may be to avoid bias in the initial examination by not introducing information perhaps believed to be contentious. Given this potential practice, one might consider a common qualification used at the end of an IME report. Sample language for such a disclaimer might include the following: "the above opinions are based upon the information that has been provided at the time of this evaluation. The opinions and impressions associated with this evaluation may be modified with any new information."

The Basis for the Claimant's Disability Includes the Effects of Pain and Fatigue on Her Functional Capacity. How do I Address these Issues with Respect to the Obtained Interpretable Testing Performance?

As described in Chapter 5, a comprehensive neuropsychological evaluation can be consistent with engaging in an all-day assessment of sedentary capacity. Claimants engage in testing from a sitting position, with minimal demands for physical activity. Opportunities for breaks, repositioning, and frequent use of writing instruments and computers may also occur. As such, an examiner has the potential to comment on observed pain-related behaviors. Further, for claims in which cognitive fatigue is asserted, an examination can contemporaneously assess any reductions in valid performance, over the course of what is often a standard workday. The assessment day, including the test administration order, planned breaks, and so on, can be optimized to assess for changes in function related to pain or fatigue. Ideally, following the completion of testing, the examiner will be in a position to comment specifically regarding the degree of cognitive demand the claimant was able to tolerate and to make any appropriate recommendations regarding work restrictions or limitations, informed not just by observation but also by test data.

The Claimant does not Evidence Any Current Cognitive or Psychiatric Impairment but is Asserting that a Return to His Occupation Would Result in the Recurrence of a Condition. How do I Address This?

For some disability claims, an individual may have recovered from his sentinel illness and regained normal functional capacity, but either the claimant or his provider is asserting that a return to all or some of the individual's prior occupational duties would result in an undue risk of recurrence.

To address such issues in the context of an IME, examiners rely on their training and expertise with respect to the base rates of recurrence of psychiatric conditions. On the whole, the available literature suggests a heightened likelihood for the recurrence of most mood-related disorders and substance use disorders, and indicates that many such conditions are chronic and are characterized by the waxing and waning of symptoms. However, many individuals do return to the workplace when they are symptomatic or when there is a heightened risk for recurrence.

A four-step model may help to address issues associated with potential risk for symptom recurrence. The first step includes completing a comprehensive evaluation to determine if remission has occurred. If current functional impairment is present, the examiner must determine what, if any, restrictions or limitations may result from such impairment. Second, the examiner should be clear about whether an opinion about risk of recurrence has been requested by the referring party. If such an opinion has been requested, it is helpful to include reference to the specific base rates for recurrence of the condition in question. The third and more difficult step in this process is to generate an understanding of what, if any, role the actual performance of the individual's occupational activities may have had in leading to the development, worsening, and/or moderating of the condition. Examiners should also be aware of the protective factors that engagement in occupational activity have in reducing or ameliorating psychiatric symptoms for many disorders (Dooley, Fielding, & Levi, 1996; Ross & Mirowsky, 1995). For some occupations, the performance of one's occupational activities can be directly related to symptom development (irregular sleep patterns or exposure to drugs of abuse). For many other occupations, there may be few if any causal links to recurrence. The fourth and final step in this process is to express any risk of recurrence in terms of an opinion related to a low or a high probability for recurrence.

What if the Claimant Takes Psychotropic or Pain Medications? Should the Testing Take Place in the Context of the Use of These Medications, or Should as-needed Medications be Withheld?

The purpose of the IME is to provide a best estimate of an individual's functional capacity and to extrapolate this data to the performance of work-related activities. As such, potential medication effects should be considered as part of the overall clinical picture. As maintenance or routine medications are likely to have some degree of consistent impact on function, if at all, claimants should remain on their standard regimen during the course of evaluation. Deviations from a standard regimen (i.e., mediations forgotten or extra dosing) should be duly noted.

The Data Obtained do not Reflect Impairment that Would Preclude the Claimant from being able to Complete Occupational Duties, but Some Sort of Workplace Accommodations Appear Indicated. What Sort of Accommodations Should I Consider?

Depending on the cognitive or psychiatric domain in which some reduction of function is present, there is a wide range of potential accommodations to consider. While the list provided in Box 7.2 is not exhaustive, examiners may

Box 7.2 Examples of Possible Workplace Accommodations for Employers

Attendance and Punctuality Issues

- Offer flexible start time
- Offer flexible schedule
- Allow work from home
- Allow part-time work schedule

Handling Stress and Emotions

- Reduce distractions in the workplace
- Establish clear and written short- and long-term performance goals
- Allow for breaks to reset emotionally
- Establish clear work schedule and expectations regarding overtime
- Divide larger assignments into smaller tasks and goals
- Ensure job is focused on essential functions

Meeting Deadlines and Staying Organized

- Assign time-intensive projects with a clearly stated deadline and have the employee acknowledge and commit to the deadline
- Provide mentoring and strategic follow-up with the employee about the progress of assignments
- Mentor and coach by direct observation

Attention and Concentration Difficulties

- Reduce distractions in the workplace
- Provide privacy/quiet area for working
- Schedule uninterrupted work time
- Allow for breaks
- Divide tasks into smaller steps
- Focus on only essential functions
- Modify or provide administrative support
- Provide a daily to-do list
- Make use of electronic reminders and alerts

Memory Difficulties

- Maintain a current calendar
- Offer an electronic calendar that provides reminders
- Make use of a scribe during meetings
- Decrease distractions
- Provide space enclosures or a private office
- Plan for uninterrupted work time
- Allow for frequent breaks
- Divide large assignments into smaller tasks and steps
- Restructure job to include only essential functions
- Provide clerical support
- Make a daily to-do list
- Provide use of electronic organizers
- Remind employee of important dates

wish to consider these as well as others, tailoring them to meet the specific needs of a given claimant and work setting.

What if the Claimant has Clearly Indicated that She is not Motivated to Return to her Occupation? How do I Separate What May be Personal Choice from Lack of Motivation Due to a Psychiatric or Neurologic Condition(s)?

The unique nature of disability policies (as opposed to many other types of disability coverage) can result in scenarios in which a claimant may present for evaluation while performing another occupation on either a full- or part-time basis. An individual may have also returned to performing her occupation on a limited or part-time basis, and at issue is her capacity to resume all or additional duties. An understanding of the context of the IME examination is critical to providing conclusions to assist in the disability determination process. While continued functional impairment may be the basis for continued occupational restrictions or limitations, the presence of choice (versus impairment) may be the most salient factor that has prevented an individual from resuming all or part of her prior occupation. There are also scenarios in which a claimant may believe that recovery has not or will not happen, and treatment or interventions that could reasonably assist in returning to her occupation have not been pursued.

A thorough review of the available records and exploration of these issues in the course of the clinical interview can shed light on the issues. This process should also lead to an understanding of the role that a treatment provider's views have played in the claimant's conclusions in this regard. If a treatment provider has articulated to the claimant that return to his prior occupation would necessarily be deleterious or that recovery is not possible, the degree to which this has shaped a claimant's understanding of his condition can be quite significant, whether factually accurate or not.

The presence of a non- or partially remitted psychiatric condition, particularly a mood disorder resulting in low motivation or negative self-bias, can make it difficult to tease apart factors resulting in a lack of motivation to attempt a return to the claimant's occupation. The presence of other factors (i.e., legal barriers, lack of any specific job to return to, significant practical burdens to restarting a business) can also be present and are worth exploring. Financial incentives may also be present and should be considered.

The Claimant has Asserted the Presence of a Condition that Only Variably Impacts his Function. How do I Address this Issue in the Course of my Examination and Report?

A fairly common complaint associated with reduced work capacity is the presence of waxing and waning symptoms that variably impact an individual's work capacity. Such variability may be asserted as becoming problematic after a few hours of cognitive effort or more distally in a reduction of function in the hours or day after the exertion of mental effort. In an evaluation that is defined by a limited period of direct contact, addressing concerns such as this requires careful consideration and at times adjustment of the assessment process.

The first step in making such a determination lies with the insurer, who should be obtaining information regarding the claimant's asserted functional capacity, both from the perspective of the treatment providers and the claimant himself or herself. Such investigation may involve peer-to-peer contact between the claimant's providers and the insurer's psychological or medical consultants to elucidate the specific limitations that are being asserted. The second step is for the insurer to clearly convey this information to the IME provider. This information should be covered in the referral letter. Frequently, the insurer will request a format for the evaluation that can address these concerns, but some may not. For example, if a claimant asserts declining attention/concentration after 2–3 hours of mental effort, the insurer may request that the evaluation be completed in a single day so that actual objective data regarding any decline in function may be obtained. Another common scenario is the assertion of accumulated fatigue and mental decline the day following any period of mental exertion. To adequately assess such an assertion, the evaluation would need to include additional contact the following day to measure such dysfunction. In the event that the referring party has not requested a specific structure for the evaluation, the IME examiner should contact the referral source immediately upon reviewing the records to identify the need to tailor the scheduling of the examination to address concerns about variability in function.

Assuming an IME examiner has established a schedule for assessment that has the potential to identify the reduction of function within the context of a single evaluation (either by extending the testing day or assessing over multiple days), it is important to develop an order of test administration that allows for the comparison of performance within a single cognitive domain at different points in the overall assessment. The structure of the evaluation should also allow for an understanding of the degree of variability that would be needed between the individual tests that can lead to a conclusion regarding functional decline. To reach these objectives, the IME examiner needs to be flexible in the order of test administration within the context of the test battery. It is important to maintain a clear understanding of the ways in which a change in the order of test administration can help to obtain reliable and valid test data and answer the referral questions.

I Have Been Asked To Provide Specific Work-related Restrictions or Limitations Based on the Data Obtained. How Do I Go About Providing a Comprehensive Answer to Such Questions?

The process of generating appropriate occupational restrictions and limitations from neuropsychological test findings is a skill developed by many neuropsychologists in the course of their routine clinical work, particularly those working in rehabilitation settings. However, depending on training, experience, or specific practice setting (which may be focused solely on differential diagnosis), it is not a skill that all neuropsychologists have. The generation of occupational restrictions and limitations first depends on an accurate understanding of a claimant's occupational duties, obtained through the course of the record review and clinical interview. Because many disability policies are based on the capacity to perform one's broader occupation versus specific job, the inclusion of a vocational analysis in the records can be valuable for gaining an understanding of the unique factors in a claimant's occupation versus his or her specific job. The clinical interview provides the opportunity to gain a better understanding of potential differences between the two, as well as identifying potential stressors or duties that may have been unique to a prior job versus the given occupation as a whole.

Another critical element in this process is having a clear understanding of the differences between restrictions and limitations (as described in Chapter 4). It is also important to differentiate between techniques that might help maximize occupational functioning and the presence of actual occupational restrictions or limitations. For example, many individuals make use of lists and reminders to optimize their efficiency in the absence of any actual memory deficit. On the other hand, an individual with a memory impairment would require the use of such compensatory strategies in order to maintain adequate occupational function. The presence of less-than-adequate approaches to work-related tasks (e.g., poor organization of the workday, failing to make use of technology to maximize performance and efficiency) may be problematic for many individuals without any functional impairment. The IME examiner should make explicit in their conclusions whether any recommendations stem from ways to optimize functioning versus those that arise from ongoing functional impairment.

In the presence of functional impairment that would likely impact occupational functioning, the inability to perform specific duties may be present. A requisite skill for IME examiners when describing occupational limitations is the ability to link functional impairments to specific duties by providing examples of ways in which the functional impairments are likely to have deleterious effects on work duties. It is generally helpful to review the occupational description provided and to make a careful consideration of the impact of any functional impairments for each listed duty. Work restrictions based on the potential for worsening of symptoms or negative impact on others (e.g., adverse outcomes for others based on poor occupational performance by health professionals) should also be considered and detailed in the IME examiner's report.

Conclusions

As noted in the preceding sections, the process of test interpretation in an independent neuropsychological evaluation may raise many issues not typically encountered in standard clinical assessments. Evaluators must be prepared to address these issues proactively in order to respond to the specific referral questions, as well as unique circumstances that may be posed in an individual independent evaluation.

8

Follow-up Issues

The neuropsychological IME typically does not end with the last test administered, nor should it. Managing post-exam interactions and the requests often made of independent examiners is an important part of overall IME process. Appropriate management of such matters strengthens the value of the IME and the specific neuropsychologist's contribution to decision-makers, whereas missteps can compromise an otherwise valuable examination.

Feedback from Examinee

Test administration is commonly the final step in the face-to-face examination process, although observations or responses that occurred during testing may prompt the neuropsychologist to ask for additional information or clarification of topics covered during the interview. Information obtained during testing may also generate questions to be asked of collateral sources or the need to pursue and review additional records. However, once the face-to-face component of the examination has been completed, it can be beneficial to obtain general feedback on the process from the examinee. The examinee should confirm that the interactions were courteous and respectful and that reasonable efforts were made to help the examinee feel comfortable, including offering breaks as needed. Typically, an appropriate informed consent process at the outset helps prepare the examinee for the experience and eliminates any significant adverse experiences. However, if the examinee perceives that the examiner did not strive to provide a courteous and respectful examination context, the examiner should be open to the feedback, attempt to correct any misconceptions, and strive to modify ways of interacting with examinees, if needed, in the future. Because examinees may change their perception of the examiner based on the content of the report, it can be very helpful to ask examinees immediately after the exam to complete a brief feedback form that documents the neuropsychologist's professional demeanor and the examinee's contentment with the process. Carone, Bush, and Iverson (2013) provide a sample examinee feedback form.

Feedback to Examinee

One important way that neuropsychological IMEs differ from clinical evaluations is that independent examiners do not provide verbal feedback or copies of reports directly to examinees. Results are provided to the retaining party and often to neuropsychological employees or consultants who work with the retaining party. Commonly, examinees or their legal representatives can obtain a copy of the report from the retaining party. This issue should be discussed with the examinee during the informed consent process, at the outset of the examination. However, if contacted directly by an examinee or an examinee's representative requesting a copy of the report or verbal feedback, the neuropsychologists should direct the person to the referral source.

The APA Ethics Code (APA, 2010; Ethical Standard 9.10, Explaining Assessment Results) notes that psychologists take reasonable steps to ensure that the results are explained to examinees or their representatives unless the examination context (e.g., forensic contexts) precludes such explanations. The *Specialty Guidelines for Forensic Psychology* (SGFP; APA, 2013) essentially restate Ethical Standard 9.10 in its section on Provision of Assessment Feedback (Guideline 10.05).

Sending Data to Consultants

Disability insurance carriers commonly employ or otherwise retain the services of neuropsychological consultants, in addition to the independent examiners that they retain for individual cases. Independent examiners are often asked to send their reports and raw test data to the neuropsychology colleague who works for the disability insurance carrier. Such colleagues are qualified to judge the appropriateness of the assessment measures and procedures, review the data for mistakes, and to judge whether the conclusions are based on empirical evidence. Therefore, it is appropriate to send the materials to the colleague. Independent examiners are typically informed of this expectation at the outset of the agreement to perform the IME.

The neuropsychology colleagues working for the insurance carrier may also request a telephone conversation with the independent examiner if issues are identified that could benefit from clarification. Such conversations are not intended to reflect dissatisfaction with the independent examiner's practices or opinions; rather, they are simply intended to gather information that the carrier can use to make appropriate decisions regarding the examinee's disability benefits. After such telephone discussions occur, the neuropsychology colleague may draft a written summary of the discussion content and send it to the independent examiner for approval or edits. The independent examiner is typically compensated for the additional expenditure of time.

Examinee Contact

In addition to occasionally being contacted by examinees requesting copies of reports, independent examiners may be contacted by examinees wishing to provide additional information or clarification of issues that were discussed or that they believe should have been discussed during the examination. In such situations, neuropsychologists should use their judgment in determining whether to have additional contact with the examinee and, if so, whether or how to use the information obtained. In addition, although the insurance carrier typically interacts with the examinee regarding scheduling the IME, sometimes examinees contact the neuropsychologist to reschedule or obtain directions. The neuropsychologist should discuss with the retaining party whether it is acceptable to reschedule directly with the examinee and, if so, inform the retaining party of the new appointment. Of course, providing directions to the location of the IME is entirely appropriate. At all times, the neuropsychologist maintains a professional demeanor that includes treating the examinee with courtesy and respect.

Handling New Information and Revising Reports

Sometimes independent examiners receive new information, via the referral source, that could potentially change the initial impressions and conclusions. Such situations offer the relatively unique opportunity to correct diagnostic errors. Although it is probably very difficult for most practitioners to admit, it is naïve to believe that any neuropsychologist over the course of a career has not misdiagnosed someone. In IME and other forensic contexts, there is often no way to know what becomes of the examinee following the IME. However, the course of missed diagnosis may emerge over time and reveal the correct diagnosis. When such information is made available to the neuropsychological examiner and an updated opinion is sought, rather than holding firm, often in a defensive manner, to the original opinion, the neuropsychologist should strive to consider the new information in an objective manner and provide an evidence-based response. Consistent with professional ethics, neuropsychologists have both an opportunity and obligation to get it right after getting it wrong (Bush & Morgan, in press).

In some circumstances, the retaining party may request that a report be modified or revised with regard to format and/or content. Although formatting changes may be reasonable, with respect to altering, adding, or omitting content and conclusions of reports, Bush, Barth, Pliskin, et al. (2005) noted that "there are very few acceptable reasons to modify reports once they have been completed . . . such requests should be considered carefully in reference to standards for objectivity. Modifications must ultimately reflect the beliefs of the neuropsychologist, not those of another party . . ." (p. 1002). It is advisable for independent examinees to retain copies of all versions of reports that have been sent to other parties.

Completion of the Case

Referral sources and independent examiners sometimes have different expectations, or a complete lack of expectations, about when the neuropsychologist's role in a given case should be considered completed. Because IME contexts frequently involve neuropsychologists being contacted for additional information or opinions or for copies of data and reports, the specific point of termination for a particular case may be difficult to determine unless both parties have identified a projected ending point. As Bush, Barth, Pliskin, et al. (2005) state, "The relationship between the neuropsychologist and the retaining third party may end when payment for services is made, when the report is submitted, or when testimony has been provided. The neuropsychologist should determine beforehand when the relationship will be considered terminated . . ." (pp. 1002–1003).

Record Retention and Handling Subpoenas

Record-keeping requirements are established by state and federal laws, and APA (2007) has provided guidelines regarding the content and maintenance of records. However, as Heilbronner and Bush (in press) note in the context of neuropsychological disability examinations, such "authoritative sources often do not differentiate between records generated and obtained as part of clinical and forensic (e.g., NDE) evaluations, resulting in a lack of clarity in the context of NDEs about which records to keep and how long to keep them." Although APA's guidelines do not mention forensic practice specifically, they do mention situations that arise in forensic practice, such as whether to re-release, in response to a subpoena, records received from other parties. Guideline 5 (Maintenance of Records) states, "when a psychologist is responding to a subpoena for 'any and all records' upon which the psychologist relied in forming opinions, it is generally necessary to re-release any third-party information included in the record. The psychologist may nevertheless provide advance notification to the client and allow sufficient time for objection to be raised before responding to such requests for records" (p. 997). Of course, in the context of IMEs, the client is the retaining party, rather than the examinee. Regarding handling subpoenas, neuropsychologists must respond to them but need not automatically comply with them. For example, an appropriate response to a subpoena issued by an attorney for a copy of the IME report would be to direct, in writing, the attorney to the referral source, reminding the attorney that the referral source is the client. In contrast to subpoenas, neuropsychologists must comply with court orders that are signed by judges. Nevertheless, when concerns about the content of a court order exist, the neuropsychologist can contact the court to express the concern and seek a compromise or other acceptable solution.

The SGFP (APA, 2013) states that psychologists should establish a system of documentation and records maintenance and, having considered the unique aspects of a given case, inform the retaining party of any limits of record-keeping duration (Guideline 10.08, Record Keeping). Independent examiners may receive voluminous records to review. Adequate description of such records in the body of the neuropsychological report precludes the need to maintain others' records for extended periods. Neuropsychologists should maintain their own reports, data, billing, and other records for a duration that is consistent with legal requirements, professional guidelines, and completion of the case, including appeals, whichever is longer. Electronic versions of records may be easily stored in perpetuity, although the possible risks of unanticipated dissemination through hacking or accidental dissemination should be considered when making decisions about maintaining records longer than is required or recommended. Maximizing the confidentiality and security of the records must be the primary consideration (APA, 2010, Ethical Standard 6.02, Maintenance, Dissemination, and Disposal of Confidential Records of Professional and Scientific Work; Bush, Naugle, & Johnson-Greene, 2002).

The SGFP (APA, 2013) states, "forensic practitioners strive to inform the retaining party of the limits of record keeping times. If requested to do so, forensic practitioners consider maintaining such records until notified that all appeals in the matter have been exhausted, or sending a copy of any unique components/aspects of the record in their care and control to the retaining party before destruction of the record" (Guideline 10.08, Record Keeping, p. 16). In the context of IMEs, neuropsychologists inform examinees during the informed consent process that they will be releasing the report only to the retaining party or its representatives, rather than to the examinee or the examinee's representatives; this practice promotes agreement among all parties from the outset so that disappointments and frustrations about this issue can be avoided following the examination.

Much has been written about whether to release raw test data and materials to non-psychologists (e.g., Bush & Martin, 2006; Bush, Rapp, & Ferber, 2010). Through its efforts to separate test data from test materials (a distinction that is artificial at best), the APA Ethics Code complicated the matter. The underlying idea is that widespread dissemination of test data and materials can be very harmful to the profession of neuropsychology and those served by neuropsychologists. Releasing test data and materials to those who do not fully appreciate the risks and are not invested in safeguarding the security of the data and materials can cause harm that far outweighs the benefit of releasing them. Neuropsychologists should willingly release test data and materials to colleagues but should take the steps needed to maximize test security (see Bush, Rapp, & Ferber, 2010).

Handling Complaints

Sometimes examinees are not pleased with the conclusions rendered by the independent neuropsychologist. For a variety of reasons, the results of the IME may not support the examinee's disability claim, resulting in considerable financial loss to the examinee. Examinees in such situations may express their disappointment and anger by filing complaints with state licensing boards, professional ethics committees, and/or organizations for which the neuropsychologist works. Although such complaints may be without merit, the neuropsychologist still must invest time, energy, and resources in responding to the complaint. Neuropsychologists position themselves well to address complaints by engaging in a thorough informed consent process, engaging in usual and customary practices, providing evidence-based conclusions, treating the examinee in a courteous and respectful manner, and having the examinee complete a feedback form at the conclusion of the IME. It is difficult for an examinee to later allege inappropriate treatment by a neuropsychologist if the examinee previously completed and signed a form stating that there were no concerns at the time of the IME. Although examinees may challenge the examiner's conclusions, the ability to produce the empirical evidence base that supports the conclusions will serve the neuropsychologist well.

Of course, some complaints are valid and justified and serve an important role in protecting the public and maintaining the integrity of the profession (American Academy of Clinical Neuropsychology, 2003). Neuropsychologists should consult their own legal counsel and/or professional liability insurance carrier when notified of a formal complaint against them.

Somewhat less formal but also frustrating, examinees who are dissatisfied with the conclusions of a neuropsychological IME sometimes post negative comments about neuropsychologists in various places on the Internet. Such negative comments or reviews may be posted on blogs, review sites for health-care professionals, or sites that list products (e.g., books or tests) that the neuropsychologist has published. Neuropsychologists are often powerless to have such reviews, no matter how ridiculous, removed. Sometimes the only recourse is to post a reasoned rebuttal to the review or to ask a broader range of clients or customers to post more balanced reviews. It is typically not advisable to respond with attacks against the person who posted the negative review or to engage in lengthy online arguments with the person.

Conclusions

The role of the independent examiner in a given case typically does not end with completion of the evaluation and submission of the report and invoice. Neuropsychologists who perform or plan to perform IMEs should anticipate extended involvement in cases, should prepare for them in advance to the extent possible, and should be prepared to negotiate additional requirements. Clarification between the neuropsychologist and the retaining party regarding the anticipated completion date or time frame is best achieved at the outset of the relationship or case. Neuropsychologists who anticipate and prepare for follow-up issues in the context of IMEs advance the interests of all involved parties.

Appendix A

Three Sample Fee Schedules for Independent Neuropsychological Evaluations

Sample A: (BILLED PER HOUR)

Service

1. Review of records, interview, testing, scoring of test data, integration and interpretation of data, and report generation $XXX.XX per hour
2. Deposition time (includes preparation) $XXX.XX per hour
3. Testimony in court $XXX.XX per hour

Please note the following:

- A $XXXX.XX retainer for each of the above services is payable at the time that they are scheduled. A retainer will be refunded with 3 full business days advance notice, minus any work time that has already been completed.
- A minimum of 5 hours will be scheduled/billed for half-day depositions, deposition preparation, or court-related testimony.
- A minimum of 8 hours will be scheduled/billed for full-day depositions, deposition preparation, or court-related testimony.
- 5 hours will be billed for prescheduled services canceled without 48 hours advance notice.

- Fees for travel will be negotiated in advance but are assumed to be portal to portal.
- Payment of any fees is independent of the outcome of the case and no contingency fee agreements are acceptable. The carrier retaining my services is ultimately responsible for any payment of forensic fees.

Please acknowledge receipt of these terms by signing and returning a copy this document.

I agree to the above terms and have the authority to act on behalf of my company to agree to the above terms and conditions.

____________________________ ______________

Printed Name Date

____

Signed Name

Fee Schedule for Independent Neuropsychological Evaluations

Sample B: (BILLED PER EXAMINATION)

Service

A full-day neuropsychological evaluation that includes a review of records (up to X hours), interview, testing, scoring of test data, integration and interpretation of data, and report generation XXX.XX per evaluation

2. Additional record review	$XXX.XX per hour
3. Deposition time (includes preparation)	$XXX.XX per hour
4. Testimony in court	$XXX.XX per hour

Please note the following:

- A $XXXX.XX retainer for each of the above services is payable at the time that they are scheduled. A retainer will be refunded with 3 full business days advance notice, minus any work time that has already been completed.
- A minimum of 5 hours will be scheduled/billed for half-day depositions, deposition preparation, or court-related testimony.
- A minimum of 8 hours will be scheduled/billed for full-day depositions, deposition preparation, or court-related testimony.
- 5 hours will be billed for prescheduled services canceled without 48 hours advance notice.
- Fees for travel will be negotiated in advance but are assumed to be portal to portal.
- Payment of any fees is independent of the outcome of the case and no contingency fee agreements are acceptable. The carrier retaining my services is ultimately responsible for any payment of forensic fees.

Please acknowledge receipt of these terms by signing and returning a copy this document.

I agree to the above terms and have the authority to act on behalf of my company to agree to the above terms and conditions.

____________________________ ______________

Printed Name Date

____

Signed Name

Fee Schedule for Independent Neuropsychological Evaluations

Sample C: Travel Expenses

In addition to the fees for evaluation services, the following fees and conditions for conducting an evaluation outside of my office include the following:

1. The retaining party is responsible for any fees associated with securing an appropriate venue for the evaluation. The preference is for a private conference room within a facility that provides such services.
2. In addition to fees for securing the room for a full day, the retaining party will be responsible for any additional fees in order to provide water or other refreshments for the claimant's use during the course of the evaluation. This does not include costs for meals.
3. The charges for my travel include $XXX.XX per hour for my travel time to and from my office to the evaluation venue. For anticipated travel of greater than X.X hours, the retaining party shall be responsible for the cost of a single room for one night.

Based on the above, the following fees are estimated for this evaluation:

Proposed location of examination: ____________________________

1. Room for examination: $XXX.XX
2. Refreshments: $XXX.XX
3. Travel time: $XXX.XX
4. Hotel stay cost: $XXX.XX

Total Estimated Cost: $____________________

Please note the following:

- A $XXXX.XX retainer for each of the above services is payable at the time that they are scheduled. A retainer will be refunded with 3 full business days advance notice, minus any non-refundable fees incurred in scheduling the examination.
- Payment of any of the above fees is independent of the outcome of the case and no contingency fee agreements are acceptable.

The carrier retaining my services is ultimately responsible for any payment of reservation-related fees.

Please acknowledge receipt of these terms by signing and returning a copy this document.

I agree to the above terms and have the authority to act on behalf of my company to agree to the above terms and conditions.

______________________________ ______________

Printed Name Date

____

Signed Name

Appendix B

Sample Informed Consent Form

Based on "Independent and Court-Ordered Forensic Neuropsychological Examinations: Official Statement of the National Academy of Neuropsychology" (Bush et al., 2005).

Referral Source

You have been referred for an independent neuropsychological examination by (INSERT NAME OF REFERRING PARTY).

Nature and Purpose

The goal of neuropsychological assessment is to determine if any changes have occurred in your attention, memory, language, problem-solving or other thinking skills. Neuropsychological assessment also includes evaluation of your psychological status, including the presence of a psychological condition.

The current examination has been requested because of your claim of neuropsychological difficulties. It is common when someone is reporting cognitive or emotional difficulties, and sees doctors for evaluation and treatment, that a disability insurance carrier will request an examination by an expert neuropsychologist of their choosing. Copies of your treatment records as well as disability related forms have been provided for my review. This neuropsychological examination will include an interview, where questions will be asked about your background and current medical symptoms. Additionally, standardized tests and other techniques may be used, including, but not limited to, asking questions about your knowledge of certain topics, reading, drawing figures and shapes, learning word lists or stories, viewing printed material, and manipulating objects. You will also be asked questions about psychological symptoms and difficulties. Your task is to answer questions as accurately as you can; for example, when discussing your problems, do not minimize significant problems, but also do not exaggerate lesser concerns. You are to give your best effort during the testing. This does not mean that you have to get every answer or problem correct, for no one ever does. However, you do have to give your best effort. Part of the examination will address the accuracy of your responses, as well as the degree of effort that you exert on the tests.

This referral is for evaluation purposes only and I will not be providing follow-up care or treatment. I will not be reviewing the results of this evaluation with you today or in the future. I have also been asked for my opinion regarding the treatment that you are receiving and will be providing an opinion in this regard. However, decisions regarding your treatment remain the decision between and your health-care providers.

Foreseeable Risks, Discomforts, and Benefits

For some individuals, neuropsychological examinations can cause fatigue, frustration, and anxiousness. An attempt will be made to help you minimize these factors. The results of this examination may either support or not support your claim. A determination regarding your eligibility for disability benefits is determined by your insurer.

If you feel unable to participate fully in this examination today, please notify me immediately. Your participation in this evaluation is voluntary and you are free to discontinue at any time.

Limits of Confidentiality

The results of this examination will be forwarded to the referring party. I have also been asked to provide copies of the test data obtained in this evaluation to __________, who is a consultant to your insurance carrier. The results of this examination will be forwarded directly to your insurance carrier. Any future release of the results will be at the discretion of your insurance carrier.

Beyond the above, I will only release confidential information about you obtained during the examination under some special circumstances that can limit confidentiality, which include, but are not limited to, (a) a statement of intent to harm yourself or others, (b) statements indicating harm or abuse of children or vulnerable adults, and (c) a subpoena from a court of law.

I have read and agree with the nature and purpose of this examination and to each of the points listed above. I have had an opportunity to clarify any questions and discuss any points of concern before signing.

Examinee Signature / Date

Witness Signature / Date

References

American Academy of Clinical Neuropsychology. (1999). American Academy of Clinical Neuropsychology policy on the use of non-doctoral level personnel in conducting clinical neuropsychological examinations. *The Clinical Neuropsychologist, 13*(4), 385.

American Academy of Clinical Neuropsychology. (2001). Policy statement on the presence of third party observers in neuropsychological assessments. *The Clinical Neuropsychologist, 15*(4), 433–439.

American Academy of Clinical Neuropsychology. (2003). Official position of the American Academy of Clinical Neuropsychology on ethical complaints made against clinical neuropsychologists during adversarial proceedings. *The Clinical Neuropsychologist, 17*(4), 443–445.

American Academy of Clinical Neuropsychology. (2007). American Academy of Clinical Neuropsychology (AACN) practice guidelines for neuropsychological assessment and consultation. *The Clinical Neuropsychologist, 21*(2), 209–231. 385.

American Educational Research Association, American Psychological Association, & National Council on Measurement in Education. (2014). *Standards for educational and psychological testing.* Washington, DC: Author.

American Psychiatric Association (2013). *Diagnostic and statistical manual of mental disorders*, 5th ed. Arlington, VA: Author.

American Psychological Association. (2007). Record keeping guidelines. *American Psychologist, G2*, 993–1004.

American Psychological Association. (2010). *Ethical principles of psychologists and code of conduct:* Retrieved November 7, 2012, from http://www.apa.org/ethics/code/index.aspx.

American Psychological Association. (2013). Specialty guidelines for forensic psychology. *American Psychologist, 68*, 7–19.

Armistead-Jehle, P., & Buican, B. (2012). Evaluation context and symptom validity test performance in a U.S. Military sample. *Archives of Clinical Neuropsychology, 27*, 828–839.

Anfang, S. A., & Wall, B. W. (2006). Psychiatric fitness for duty evaluations. *Psychiatric Clinics of North America, 29*(3), 675–693.

Attix, D. K., Donders, J., Johnson, Green, D., Grote, C. L., Harris, J. G., & Bauer, R. M. (2007). Disclosure of neuropsychological test data: Official position of Division 40 (Clinical Neuropsychology) of the American Psychological Association, Association of Postdoctoral Programs in Clinical Neuropsychology, and the American Academy of Clinical Neuropsychology. *The Clinical Neuropsychologist, 21*(2), 232–238.

Baum, K. (2005). Independent medical examinations: An expanding source of physician liability. *Annals of Internal Medicine, 142*(12, Pt. 1), 974–978,

Baxter v. Temple, No. 2007-0102 (State of New Hampshire Supreme Court). Retrieved from http://theaacn.org/position_papers/Baxter_v_Temple.pdg.

Benge, J. F., Pastorek, N. J., & Thornton, G. M. (2009). Postconcussive symptoms in OEF-OIF veterans: Factor structure and impact of posttraumatic stress. *Rehabilitation Psychology, 54*, 270–278.

Ben-Porath, Y. S., & Tellegen, A. (2008). *MMPI-2-RF: Manual for administration, scoring, and interpretation*. Minneapolis: University of Minnesota Press.

Bennett, B. E., Bricklin, P. M., Harris, E., Knapp, S., VandeCreek, L., & Younggren, J. N. (2006). *Assessing and managing risks in psychological practice: An individualized approach*. Rockville, MD: The Trust.

Berthelson, L., Mulchan, S. S., Odland, A. P., Miller, L. J., & Mittenberg, W. (2013). False positive diagnosis of malingering due to the use of multiple effort tests. *Brain Injury, 27*, 909–916.

Biddle, J., Roberts, K., Rosenman, K. D., & Welch, E. M. (1998). What percentage of workers with work-related illnesses receive workers' compensation benefits? *Journal of Occupational and Environmental Medicine, 142*(12, Pt. 1), 974–978.

Binder, L. M., Iverson, G. L., & Brooks, B. L. (2009). To err is human: "Abnormal" neuropsycholgoical scores and variability are common in healthy adults. *Archives of Clinical Neuropsychology, 24*(1), 31–46.

Boone, K. B. (Ed.) (2007). *Assessment of feigned cognitive impairment: A neuropsychological perspective*. New York: Guilford.

Boone, K. B. (2013). *Clinical practice of forensic neuropsychology: An evidence-based approach*. New York: Guilford Press.

Bornstein, R. A. (1985). Normative data on selected neuropsychological measures from a nonclinical sample. *Journal of Clinical Psychology, 41*, 651–659.

British Psychological Society. (2009). *Assessment of effort in clinical testing of cognitive functioning for adults*. Leicester, UK: Author.

Bruns, D., & Disorbio, J. M. (2014). The psychological evaluation of patients with chronic pain: A review of BHI 2 clinical and forensic interpretive considerations. *Psychological Injury and Law, 7*, 335–361.

Bush, S. S. (2007) *Ethical decision making in clinical neuropsychology*. New York: Oxford Press.

Bush, S. S. (2009). Symptom validity assessment practices: Ethical and professional considerations [Die praxis der beschwerdenvalidierung: Ethische und fachwissenschaftliche gesichtspunkte]. In T. Merten & H. Dettenborn (Eds.), *Assessment of malingering [Diagnostik der Beschwerdenvaliditat]* (pp. 79–100). Berlin: Deutscher Psychologen Verlag.

Bush, S. S. (2010). Determining whether or when to adopt new versions of psychological and neuropsychological tests. *The Clinical Neuropsychologist, 24*, 7–16.

Bush, S. S. (2013). Ethical considerations in mild traumatic brain injury cases and symptom validity assessment. In D. A. Carone & S. S. Bush (Eds.), *Mild traumatic brain injury: Symptom validity assessment and malingering* (pp. 45–56). New York: Springer.

Bush, S. S. (2014). Assessing symptom and performance validity in veterans. In S. S. Bush (Ed.), *Psychological assessment of veterans* (pp. 433–452). New York: Oxford University Press.

Bush, S. S., Barth, J. T., Pliskin, N. H., Arffa, S., Axelrod, B. N., Blackburn, L. B., . . . Silver, C. H. (2005a). Independent and court-ordered forensic neuropsychological examinations: Official Statement of the National Academy of Neuropsychology. *Archives of Clinical Neuropsychology, 20*, 997–1007.

Bush, S. S., Connell, M. A., & Denney, R. L. (2006). *Ethical practice in forensic psychology: A systematic model for decision making*. Washington, DC: American Psychological Association.

Bush, S. S., Demakis, G. J., & Rohling, M. L. (Eds.) (in press). *APA handbook of forensic neuropsychology*. Washington, DC: American Psychological Association.

Bush, S. S., & Graver, C. (2013). Symptom validity assessment of military and veteran populations following mild traumatic brain injury. In D. A. Carone & S. S. Bush (Eds.), *Mild traumatic brain injury: Symptom validity assessment and malingering* (pp. 381–397). New York: Springer.

Bush, S. S., & Heilbronner, R. L. (2012). The neuropsychological IME. In S. S. Bush & G. L. Iverson (Eds.), *Neuropsychological assessment of work-related injuries* (pp. 280–302). New York: Guilford Press.

Bush, S. S., Heilbronner, R. L., & Ruff, R. M. (2014). Psychological assessment of symptom and performance validity, response bias, and malingering: Official position of the Association for Psychological Advancement in Psychological Injury and Law. *Psychological Injury and Law, 7*, 197–205.

Bush, S. S., & Martin, T. A. (2006). The ethical and clinical practice of disclosing raw test data: Addressing the ongoing debate. *Applied Neuropsychology, 13*(2), 115–124

Bush, S. S., & Martin, T. A. (2010). Privacy, confidentiality, and privilege in forensic neuropsychology. In A. M. Horton, Jr., & L. C. Hartlage (Eds.), *Handbook of forensic neuropsychology*, 2nd Eed. (pp. 235–244). New York: Springer.

Bush, S. S., & Morgan, J. (in press). Ethical practice in forensic neuropsychology. In S. S. Bush, G. J. Demakis, & M. L. Rohling (Eds.), *APA handbook of forensic neuropsychology*. Washington, DC: American Psychological Association Press.

Bush, S., Naugle, R., & Johnson-Greene, D. (2002). The interface of information technology and neuropsychology: Ethical issues and recommendations. *The Clinical Neuropsychologist, 16*, 536–547.

Bush, S. S., Pimental, P. A., Ruff, R. M., Iverson, G. L., Barth, J. T., & Broshek, D. K. (2009). Secretive recording of neuropsychological testing and interviewing: Official position of the National Academy of Neuropsychology. *Archives of Clinical Neuropsychology, 24*, 1–2.

Bush, S. S., Rapp, D. L., & Ferber, P. S. (2010). Maximizing test security in forensic neuropsychology. In A. M. Horton, Jr., & L. C. Hartlage (Eds.), *Handbook of forensic neuropsychology*, 2nd ed. (pp. 177–195). New York: Springer.

Bush, S. S., Ruff, R. M., Troster, A. I., Barth, J. T., Koffler, S. P., Pliskin, N. H., Reynolds, C. R., & Silver, C. H. (2005b). Symptom validity assessment: Practice issues and medical necessity. *Archives of Clinical Neuropsychology, 20*, 419–426.

Bush, S. S., & Schatz, P. (in press). Advanced technology and assessment: Ethical and methodological considerations. In T. D. Parsons & R. Kane (Eds.), *The role of technology in clinical neuropsychology*. New York: Oxford University Press.

Butcher, J. N., Dahlstrom, W. G., Graham, J. R., Tellegen, A., & Kaemmer, B. (1989). *Minnesota Multiphasic Personality Inventory-2 (MMPI–2): Manual for administration and scoring*. Minneapolis: University of Minnesota Press.

California Workers' Compensation Institute. (1990). *Mental stress claims in California Workers' Compensation: Incidence, costs, and trends*. San Francisco: Author.

Carone, D. A., & Bush, S. S. (Eds.) (2013). *Mild traumatic brain Injury: Symptom validity assessment and malingering*. New York: Springer.

Carone, D. A., Bush, S. S., & Iverson, G. L. (2013). Providing feedback on symptom validity, mental health, and treatment in mild traumatic brain injury. In D. A. Carone & S. S. Bush (Eds.), *Mild traumatic brain injury: Symptom validity assessment and malingering* (pp. 101–118). New York: Springer.

Chafetz, M. D. (2008). Malingering on the Social Security disability consultative examination: Predictors and base rates. *The Clinical Neuropsychologist, 22*, 529–546.

Chafetz, M. D., & Underhill, J. (2013). Estimated costs of malingered disabiltiy. *Archives of Clinical Neuropsychology, 28*(7), 633–639.

Cicerone, K. D., & Kalmar, K. (1995). Persistent postconcussion syndrome: The structure of subjective complaints after mild traumatic brain injury. *Journal of Head Trauma Rehabilitation, 10*, 1–17.

Council for Disability Awareness (2014). 2104 Long Term Disability claims review. Portland, ME. Retrieved Sep, 22, 2016 from http://disabilitycanhappen.org/research/CDA_LTD_Claims_Survey_2014.pdf.

Cox, F. H. (1949). *The oldest accident office in the world: Being the story of the Railway Passengers Assurance Company, 1849–1949.* London: Fanfare Press.

Davis, J. J., & Millis, S. R. (2014). Examination of performance validity test failure in relation to number of tests administered. *Clinical Neuropsychologist, 28*, 199–214.

Denning, J. H. (2012). The efficiency and accuracy of the Test of Memory Malingering trial 1, errors on the first 10 items of the test of memory malingering, and five embedded measures in predicting invalid test performance. *Archives of Clinical Neuropsychology, 27*, 417–432.

Direnfeld, D. M., & Roberts, J. E. (2006). Mood congruent memory in dysphoria: The role of state affect and cognitive style. *Behavior Research and Therapy, 44*(9), 1275–1285.

Dooley, D., Fielding, J., & Levi, L. (1996). Health and unemployment. *Annual Review of Public Health, 17*, 449–465.

Duff, K., & Fisher, J. M. (2005). Ethical dilemmas with third party observers. *Journal of Forensic Neuropsychology, 4*(2), 65–82.

Elias, M. F., Podraza, A. M., Pierce, M. A., & Robbins, M. A. (1990). Determining neuropsychological cut scores for older, healthy adults. *Experimental Aging Research, 16*, 209–220.

Erickson, W., Lee, C., von Schrader, S. (2015). *Disability statistics from the 2013 American Community Survey (ACS).* Ithaca, NY: Cornell University Employment and Disability Institute (EDI). Retrieved October 7, 2015, from www.disabilitystatistics.org.

Faust, D. (Ed.) (2012). *Coping with psychiatric and psychological testimony.* New York: Oxford.

Fox, D. D. (2011). Symptom validity test failure indicates invalidity of neuropsychological tests. *The Clinical Neuropsychologist, 25*, 488–495.

Franche, R. L., Frank, J., & Krause, N. (2005). Prediction of occupational disability. In I. Z. Schultz & R. J. Gatchel (Eds.), *Handbook of complex occupational disability claims* (pp. 93–116). New York: Springer.

Frederick, R. I., & Crosby, R. D. (2000). Development and validation of the Validity Indicator Profile. *Law and Human Development, 24*, 59–82.

Gavett, B. F., Lync, J. K., & McCaffrey, R. J. (2006). Third party observers: The effect size is greater than you might think. *Journal of Forensic Neuropsychology, 4*(2), 49–64.

Gervais, R. O., Green, P., Allen, L. M., III, & Iverson, G. L. (2001). Effects of coaching on symptom validity testing in chronic pain patients presenting for disability assessments. *Journal of Forensic Neuropsychology, 2*, 1–19.

Green, P. (2003). *Memory Complaints Inventory.* Edmonton, Alberta: Green's Publishing.

Green, P. (2005). *Medical Symptom Validity Test.* Edmonton, Alberta: Green's Publishing.

Green, P. (2007). The pervasive influence of effort on neuropsychological tests. *Physical Medicine and Rehabilitation Clinics of North America, 18*, 43–68.

Green, P., Allen, L. M., & Astner, K. (1996). *The Word Memory Test: A User's Guide to the Oral and Computer-Administered Forms, US Version 1.1.* Durham, NC: CogniSyst.

Green, P., Rohling, M. L., Lees-Haley, P. R., & Allen, L. M., III. (2001). Effort has a greater effect on test scores than severe brain injury in compensation claimants. *Brain Injury, 15*, 1045–1060.

Greiffenstein, M. F., Baker, W. J., & Johnson-Greene, D. (2002). Actual versus self-reported scholastic achievement of litigating postconcussion and severe closed head injury claimants. *Psychological Assessment 14*(2), 202–208.

Grote, C. L., Lewin, J. L., Sweet, J. J., & van Gorp, W. G. (2000). Responses to perceived unethical practices in clinical neuropsychology: Ethical and legal considerations. *The Clinical Neuropsychologist, 14*(1), 119–134.

Guidotti, T. L. (2003). Evidence-based medical dispute resolution. In S. L. Demmer & B. J. Gunnar (Eds.), *Disability evaluation* (pp. 86–94). Washington, DC: American Medical Association.

Guilmette, T. J. (2013). The role of clinical judgment in symptom validity assessment. In D. A. Carone & S. S. Bush (Eds.), *Mild traumatic brain injury: Symptom validity assessment and malingering* (pp. 31–43). New York: Springer.

Gunner, J. H., Miele, A. S., Lynch, J. K., & McCaffrey, R. J. (2012). The Albany Consistency Index for the Test of Memory Malingering. *Archives of Clinical Neuropsychology, 27*, 1–9.

Hadjistavropoulos, T., & Bieling, P. (2001). File review consultation in the adjudication of mental health and chronic pain disabilty claims. *Consulting Psychology: Practice and Research, 53*, 52–63.

Heaton, R. K. (2004). *Revised comprehensive norms for an expanded Halstead-Reitan battery: Demographically adjusted neuropsychological norms for African American and Caucausian adults.* Odessa, FL: Psychological Assessmetn Resources.

Heaton, R. K. Grant, I., & Matthews, C. G. (1991). *Comprehensive norms for an expanded Halstead-Reitan battery: Demographic corrections, research findings, and clinical applications.* Odessa, FL: Psychological Assessment Resources.

Heilbronner, R. L. (Ed.) (2005). *Forensic neuropsychology casebook.* New York: Guilford Press.

Heilbronner, R. L., & Bush, S. S. (in press). Neuropsychological evaluations in disability determinations. In S. S. Bush, G. J. Demakis, & M. L. Rohling (Eds.), *APA handbook of forensic neuropsychology.* Washington, DC: American Psychological Association Press.

Heilbronner, R. L., Sweet, J. J., Attix, D. K., Krull, K. R., Henry, G. K., & Hart, R. P. (2010). Official position of the American Academy of Clinical Neuropsychology on serial neuropsychological assessments: The utility and challenges of repeat test administration in clinical and forensic contexts. *The Clinical Neuropsychologist, 24*(8), 1267–1278.

Heilbronner, R. L., Sweet, J. J., Morgan, J. E., Larrabee, G. J., Millis, S. R., & Conference Participants. (2009). AACN consensus conference statement on the neuropsychological assessment of effort, response bias, and malingering. *The Clinical Neuropsychologist, 23*(7), 1093–1129.

Henry, B., Moffit, T. E., Caspi, A., Langly, J., & Silva, P. A. (1994). On the remembrance of things past: A longitudinal evaluation of the retrospective method. *Psychological Assessment, 6*, 92–101.

Hilsabeck, R. C., Gouvier, W. D., & Bolter, J. F. (1998). Reconstructive memory bias in recall of neuropsychological symptomatology. *Journal of Clinical and Experimental Neuropsychology, 20*(3), 328–338.

Holdnack, J. A., & Drozdick, L. W. (2009). *Advanced clinical solutions for the WAIS-IV and WMS-IV: Clinical and interpretive manual*. San Antonio, TX: Pearson.

Holdnack, J. A., Drozdick, L. W., Weiss, L. G., & Iverson, G. L. (Eds.) (2013). *WAIS-IV, WMS-IV and ACS: Advanced clinical interpretation*. San Diego, CA: Elsevier.

Horton, A. M., Jr., & Hartlage, L. C. (2010). *Handbook of forensic neuropsychology*, 2nd ed. New York: Springer.

Howe, L. S., & McCaffrey, R. J. (2010). Third party observation during neuropsychological evaluation: An update on the literature, practical advice for practitioners, and future directions. *The Clinical Neuropsychologist, 24*, 518–537.

Hoy-Watkins, M., Bush, S. S., & Sesta, J. J. (in press). Education and training in forensic neuropsychology. In S. S. Bush, G. J. Demakis, & M. L. Rohling (Eds.), *APA handbook of forensic neuropsychology*. Washington, DC: American Psychological Association Press.

Hurrell, J. J., Jr., & Murphy, L. R. (1996). Occupational stress intervention. *American Journal of Industrial Medicine, 29*(4), 338–341.

Iverson, G. L. (2008). Assessing for exaggeration, poor effort, and malingering in neuropsychological assessment. In A. M. Horton, Jr., & D. Wedding. (Eds.), *Neuropsychology handbook*, 3rd ed. (pp. 125–182). New York: Springer.

Iverson, G. L., Brooks, B. L., & Holdnack, J. A. (2012). Evidence-based neuropsychological assessment following work-related injury. In S. S. Bush & G. L. Iverson (Eds.), *Neuropsychological assessment of work-related injuries* (pp. 360–400). New York: Guilford Press.

Iverson, G. L., Le Page, J., Koehler, B. E., Shojania, K., & Badii, M. (2007). Test of Memory Malingering (TOMM) scores are not affected by chronic pain or depression in patients with fibromyalgia. *The Clinical Neuropsychologist, 21*, 532–546.

Johnson-Greene, D., Hardy-Morias, C., Adams, K. M., Hardy, C., & Bergloff, P. (1997). Informed consent and neuropsychological assessment: Ethical considerations and proposed guidelines. *The Clinical Neuropsychologist, 11*(4), 454–460.

Joint Commission. (2008). Behaviors that undermine a culture of safety. *Sentinel Event Alert, Issue 40*, July 9, 2008. Retrieved October 7, 2015, from http://www.jointcommission.org/assets/1/18/SEA_40.PDF.

Judd, T., Capetillo, D., Carrion-Baralt, J., Marmol, L. M., San Miguel-Montes, L., Navarrete, M. G., & Silver, C. H. (2009). Professional considerations for improving the neuropsychological evaluation of Hispanics: A National Academy of Neuropsychology Education Paper. *Archives of Clinical Neuropsychology, 24*, 127–135.

Kaufmann, P. M. (2009). Protecting raw data and psychological tests from wrongful disclosure: A primer on the law and other persuasive strategies. *The Clinical Neuropsychologist, 23*(7), 1130–1159.

Lange, R. T., Iverson, G. L., Brooks, B. L., & Rennison, V. L. (2010). Influence of poor effort on self-reported symptoms and neurocognitive test performance following mild traumatic brain injury. *Journal of Clinical and Experimental Neuropsychology, 32*, 961–972.

Larrabee, G. J. (2005). Assessment of malingering. In G. J. Larrabee (Ed.), *Forensic neuropsychology: A scientific approach* (pp. 115–158). New York: Oxford University Press.

Larrabee, G. J. (2007a). Evaluation of exaggerated health and injury symptomatology. In G. J. Larrabee (Ed.), *Assessment of malingered neuropsychological deficits.* (pp. 264–286). New York: Oxford University Press.

Larrabee, G. J. (Ed.) (2007b). *Assessment of malingered neurocognitive deficits.* New York: Oxford University Press.

Larrabee, G. J. (2008). Aggregating across multiple indicators improves the detection of malingering: Relationship to likelihood ratios. *The Clinical Neuropsychologist, 22*, 666–679.

Larrabee, G. J. (2012). *Forensic neuropsychology: A scientific approach*, 2nd ed. New York: Oxford University Press.

Larrabee, G. (2012). Performance validity and symptom validity in neuropsychological assessment. *Journal of the International Neuropsychological Society, 18*, 625–630.

Lovejoy, D. W., & Oakes, H. J. (2012). The behavioral health provider as a participant in the disability determination process: Evaluations, terminology, and systems. In S. S. Bush & G. L. Iverson (Eds.), *Neuropsychological assessment of work-related injuries* (pp. 321–343). New York: Guilford Press.

Lynch, J. K. (2005). Effect of a third party observer on neuropsychological test performance following closed head injury. *Journal of Forensic Neuropsychology, 4*(2), 17–25.

Martin, P. K., Schroeder, R. W., & Odland, A. P. (2015). Neuropsychologists' validity testing beliefs and practices: A survey of North American professionals. *The Clinical Neuropsychologist, 29*, 741–776.

McCaffrey, R. J. (guest editor) (2005). Third party observers. *Journal of Forensic Neuropsychology, 4* (2), special issue.

Meyers, J. E., & Volbrecht, M. E. (2003). A validation of multiple malingering detection methods in a large clinical sample. *Archives of Clinical Neuropsychology, 18*, 261–276.

Meyers, J. E., Volbrecht, M., Axelrod, B. N., & Reinsch-Boothby, L. (2011). Embedded symptom validity tests and overall neuropsychological test performance. *Archives of Clinical Neuropsychology, 26*, 8–15.

Miller, J. B., Axelrod, B. N., Schutte, C., & Davis, J. J. (in press). Symptom and performance validity assessment in forensic neuropsychology. In S. S. Bush, G. J. Demakis, & M. L. Rohling (Eds.), *APA handbook of forensic neuropsychology*. Washington, DC: American Psychological Association.

Morey, L. C. (1991). *Personality Assessment Inventory*. Lutz, FL: PAR.

Morgan, J. E., & Sweet, J. J. (Eds.), (2009). *Neuropsychology of malingering casebook*. New York: Taylor & Francis (Psychology Press).

Murray, C. J., & Lopez, A. D. (Eds.). (1996). *The global burden of disease and injury series*, volume 1: *A comprehensive assessment of mortality and disability from diseases, injuries and risk factors in 1990 and projected to 2020*. Cambridge, MA: Harvard University Press.

National Academy of Neuropsychology. (2000a) Presence of third party observers during neuropsychological testing. *Archives of Clinical Neuropsychology, 15*(5), 379–380.

National Academy of Neuropsychology. (2000b). The use of neuropsychology test technicians in clinical practice. *Archives of Clinical Neuropsychology, 15*(5), 381–382.

National Academy of Neuropsychology Policy and Planning Committee. (2003). *Test security: An update. Official Statement of the National Academy of Neuropsychology*. Retrieved September 7, 2012, from http://www.nanonline.org/docs/PAIC/PDFs/ANATestSecurityUpdate.pdf.

Oakes, H. J., Lovejoy, D. W., Tartar, S., & Holdnack, J. A. (2013). Understanding index and subtest scatter in healthy adults. In J. A. Holdnack, Drozdick, L, Weiss, L. G., & Iverson, G. I. (Eds.), *WAIS-IV, WMS-V, and ACS: Advanced clinical interpretation* (pp. 103–169). New York: Elsevier.

Orsini, D. L. Van Gorp, W. G., & Boone, K. B. (1988). *The neuropsychology casebook*. New York: Springer-Verlag.

Palmer, B. W., Boone, K. B., Lesser, I. M., & Wohl, M. A. (1998). Base rates of "impaired" neuropsychological test performance among healthy older adults. *Archives of Clinical Neuropsychology, 13*(6), 503–511.

Piechowski, L. D. (2006). Forensic consultation in disability insurance matters. *Journal of Psychiatry and Law, 34*, 151–167.

Piechowski, L. D. (2015). Identifying examiner-related threats to validity in the forensic assessment of disability. *International Journal of Law and Psychiatry*, http://dx.doi.org/10.1016/j.ijlp.2015.08.010.

Puente, A. E., Adams, R., Barr, W. B., Bush, S. S., & NAN Policy and Planning Committee. (2006). The use, education, training and supervision of neuropsychological test technicians (psychometrists) in clinical practice: Official statement of the National Academy of Neuropsychology. *Archives of Clinical Neuropsychology, 21*, 837–839.

Rabin, L. A., Barr, W. B., & Burton, L. A. (2005). Assessment practices of clinical neuropsychologists in the United States and Canada: A survey of INS, NAN, and APA Division 40 members. *Archives of Clinical Neuropsychology, 20*, 33–65.

Rey, A. (1941). The psychological examination in cases of traumatic encepholopathy. Problems. *Archives de Psychologie, 28*, 215–285.

Richman, J., Green, P., Gervais, R., Flaro, L., Merten, T., Brockhaus, R., et al. (2006). Objective tests of symptom exaggeration in independent medical examinations. *Journal of Occupational and Environmental Medicine, 48*(3), 303–311.

Rogler, L. H. Malgady, R. G., & Tyron, W. W. (1992). Evaluation of mental health: Issues of memory in the Diagnostic Interview Schedule. *Journal of Nervous and Mental Disease, 180*(4), 215–222; discussion 223–226.

Rohling, M. J., Miller, R. M., Axelrod, B. N., Wall, J. R., Lee, A. J., Kinikini, D. T. (2015). Is co-norming required? *Archives of Clinical Neuropsychology, 30*, 611–633.

Ross, C. E., & Mirowsky, J. (1995). Does employment affect health? *Journal of Health and Social Behavior, 36*, 230–243.

Rostow, C. D., & Davis, R. D. (2004). *A handbook for psychological fitness-for-duty evaluations in law enforcement*. Binghamton, NY: Haworth Press.

Sharland, M. J., & Gfeller, J. D. (2007). A survey of neuropsychologists' beliefs and practices with respect to the assessment of effort. *Archives of Clinical Neuropsychology, 22*, 213–223.

Sherman, E. M. S., & Brooks, B. L. (2012). *Pediatric forensic neuropsychology*. New York: Oxford University Press.

Simon, G. E., & VonKorff, M. (1995). Recall of psychiatric history in cross-sectional surveys: Implications for epidemiologic research. *Epidemiologic Reviews, 17*(1), 221–227.

Slick, D. J., & Sherman, E. M. S. (2013). Differential diagnosis of malingering. In D. A. Carrone & S. S. Bush (Eds.), *Mild traumatic brain injury: Symptom validity assessment and malingering* (pp. 57–72). New York: Springer.

Slick, D. J., Sherman, E. M. S., & Iverson, G. L. (1999). Diagnostic criteria for malingered neurocognitive dysfunction: Proposed standards for clinical practice and research. *Clinical Neuropsychologist, 13*, 545–561.

Soble, J. R., Silva, M. A., Vanderploeg, R. D., Curtis, G., Belanger, H. G., Donnell, A. J., & Scott, S. G. (2014). Normative data for the Neurobehavioral Symptom Inventory and post-concussion symptom profiles among TBI, PTSD, and nonclinical samples. *The Clinical Neuropsychologist, 28*, 614–632.

Steinmeyer, C. H. (1986). A meta-analysis of Halstead-Reitan test performances of non-brain damaged subjects. *Archives of Clinical Neuropsychology, 1*, 301–307.

Stucky, K. J., & Bush, S.S. (2017). *The Neuropsychology Fact-Finding Casebook: A Training and Study Resource*. New York: Oxford University Press.

Sweet, J. J. (Ed.). (1999). *Forensic neuropsychology: Fundamentals and practice*. Lisse, The Netherlands: Swets & Zeitlinger.

Sweet, J. J., Meyer, D. G., Nelson, N. W., & Moberg, P. J. (2011). The TCN/AACN 2010 "Salary Survey": Professional practices, beliefs and incomes of U.S. neuropsychologists. *The Clinical Neuropsychologist, 25*, 12–61.

Tombaugh, T. (1996). *Test of Memory Malingering*. North Tonawanda, NY: Multi-Health Systems.

US Department of Veterans Affairs. (2011). *Veterans Benefits Administration annual benefits reports, 1985–2012*. Office of Policy & Planning, Office of the Actuary. Retrieved October 7, 2015, from http://www.va.gov/vetdata/docs/QuickFacts/SCD_quickfacts_FY2014.pdf.

US Social Security Administration (2003). Facts & figures about Social Security. Retrieved on December 26, 2016 from https://www.ssa.gov/policy/docs/chartbooks/fast_facts/2003

US Social Security Administration. (2015). *Selected data from Social Security's Disability Program*. Retrieved October 7, 2015, from http://www.ssa.gov/oact/STATS/dibStat.html.

US Publishing Office. (2006). United States Code, Supplement 5, Title 42. Retrieved October 7, 2015, from http://www.gpo.gov/fdsys/granule/USCODE-2011-title42/USCODE-2011-title42-chap7-subchapII-sec42.

Van Dyke, S. K., Millis, S. R., Axelrod, B. N., & Hanks, R. A. (2013). Assessing effort: Differentiating performance and symptom validity. *The Clinical Neuropsychologist, 27*, 1234–1246.

van Impelen, A., Merckelbach, H., Jelicic, M., & Merten, T. (2014). The Structured Inventory of Malingered Symptomatology (SIMS): A systematic review and meta-analysis. *Clinical Neuropsychologist, 28*, 1336–1365.

Vanderploeg, R. D., Cooper, D. B., Belanger, H. G., Donnell, A. J., Kennedy, J. E., Hopewell, C. A., & Scott, S. G. (2014). Screening for postdeployment conditions: Development and cross-validation of an embedded validity scale in the neurobehavioral symptom inventory. *Journal of Head Trauma Rehabilitation, 29*(1), 1–10.

Victor, T. L., Boone, K. B., Serpa, J. G., Buehler, J., & Ziegler, E. A. (2009). Interpreting the meaning of multiple symptom validity test failure. *Clinical Neuropsychologist, 23*, 297–313.

Vore, D. A. (2007) The disabilty psychological independent medical evaluation: Case law, ethical issues and procedures. In A. Goldstein (Ed.), *Forensic psychology: Emerging topics and expanding roles* (pp. 489–510). Hoboken, NJ: Wiley.

Waldron, C. (2003). Trends in morbidity: Pricing and reserving individual disability insurance is no walk in the park. *The Actuary, 37*(6), 7–8, 15.

Warren, P. A. (2005). *The management of workplace mental health issues and appropriate disability prevention strategies*. San Diego, CA: Work Loss Data Institute.

Wechsler, D. (2008a). *Wechsler Adult Intelligence Scale*, 4th ed. San Antonio, TX: Psychological Corporation.

Wechsler, D. (2008b). *Wechsler Memory Scale*, 4th ed. San Antonio, TX: Pearson.

Widom, C. S., & Morris, S. (1997). Accuracy of adult recollections of childhood victimization, Part 2: Childhood sexual abuse. *Psychological Assessment, 9*(1), 34–46.

Widows, M. R., & Smith, G. P. (2005). *Structured Interview of Malingering Symptomatology (SIMS)*. Lutz, FL: PAR.

Youngjohn, J. R. (1995). Confirmed attorney coaching prior to neuropsychological evaluation. *Assessment, 2*, 279–283.

Index

Note: Page numbers followed by b or *t* indicate a box or table on the designated page